RAP
THERAPY

D1383451

RAP THERAPY

A Practical Guide for Communicating with Youth and Young Adults Through Rap Music

DON ELLIGAN, PH.D

KENSINGTON PUBLISHING CORP.
www.kensingtonbooks.com

DAFINA BOOKS are published by

Kensington Publishing Corp.
850 Third Avenue
New York, NY 10022

Copyright © 2004 Don Elligan

All rights reserved. No part of this book may be reproduced in any form or by
any means without the prior written consent of the publisher, excepting brief
quotes used in reviews.

All Kensington titles, imprints, and distributed lines are available at special
quantity discounts for bulk purchases for sales promotions, premiums, fund-
raising, educational, or institutional use. Special book excerpts or customized
printings can also be created to fit specific needs. For details, write or phone
the office of the Kensington special sales manager: Kensington Publishing
Corp., 850 Third Avenue, New York, NY 10022, attn: Special Sales Department; phone 1-800-221-2647.

Dafina Books and the Dafina logo are Reg. U.S. Pat. & TM Off.

First printing: April 2004

10 9 8 7 6 5 4 3 2 1

Printed in the United States of America

ISBN 0-7582-0396-9

Contents

Preface

HAVE you ever questioned yourself, a friend, or a colleague: "How am I ever going to get through to this kid?" Have you ever wondered: "Why does my child like listening to rap music so much?" Have you ever thought: "I have to get this rap music away from my child because it is going to ruin his life"?

We live in a media-driven world where entertainers have a significant influence on our cultural identity, norms, and beliefs. These messages in songs and music videos can be even more influential for the impressionable minds of today's youth. Music has historically been a source of significant influence on youth of different cultures, classes, and gender. Rap music has become one of the most popular and lucrative forms of music today. Its presence is everywhere. Likewise, it has become one of the most impressionable on the developmental psychology of youth. The purpose of this book is to help parents, educators, therapists, and others interested in the influence of rap music on youth and young adults to understand how to utilize rap music for positive and constructive communication. This book will help one learn how to manage rap music's influence on youth and identify potential themes that can be taught through the use of rap music.

My impetus to develop "rap therapy" was in part the result of my observation of how many of the young clients I work with are influenced by the culture of hip-hop and rap music. Many young clients return to my office week after week reciting the lyrics of their favorite rap song and dressed in their favorite hip-hop outfit. I soon realized that rap music not only influenced their social life, but it had also diffused into their language, dress, behavior, thoughts, and perceptions. Furthermore, by utilizing their interest in rap, I soon realized and became fascinated by the level of insight that rap music could give me into the psychology of youth captivated by its appeal. I soon began to look at rap music as an anchor in my therapeutic relationship and work with those youth and young adults who are part of the rap and hip-hop culture. Many of the lyrics that clients would come into my office reciting, lyrics that I once took for granted and assumed to be a youthful whim, were in many cases the single most important metaphor for their challenges, conflicts, and fantasies. With this in mind, I began to analyze critically the relationship of the particular rap song a client would come into my office reciting in relation to his or her psychological issues. It soon became clear that it was not by coincidence that a young boy who had been involved in several incidents of sexual misbehavior would come in singing "Grinding" by the Neptunes and Clipses. Not only can rap music give one a glimpse into the challenges many youth are confronted with, but it can also be seen as a place of strength as opposed to a pathological interest promoting negative behaviors and beliefs. An interest in rap music can be seen as a strength that many youth have that is often overlooked and not utilized by those working with them to promote positive change in their lives.

I have found that rap therapy provides a way to harness my clients' inherent strengths so that they work in their favor and not their disfavor. When a rap star wears hip-hop gear to court and the jury finds him or her guilty, this can become a topic of discussion and education with youth to learn about the politics of interpersonal relations. In this dialogue, the conversation does not focus on the prohibition of wearing the type of clothes they like, but rather when is it an appropriate and inappropriate time to wear their favorite outfit and the potential consequences of not having this level of insight.

Furthermore, the use of rap music in therapy, education, or a dialogue allows one to speak to youth and young adults from an area of familiarity and acceptance of their environmental circumstances. This can promote a better working relationship with them.

In this book, rap therapy is described in such a way that concerned adults can begin to make rap music work for them in their conversations with youth influenced by rap music. Rap music can become another source of conversation with youth to help teach and educate them about many aspects of life. This book will review the stories of different youth and young adults who have benefited from using rap music as a tool to promote greater insight and self-awareness and as an education for many of life's struggles.

In chapter 1, rap therapy will be introduced through the use of a brief case presentation and overview. Chapter 2 will give a brief overview of adolescent development and some of the challenges confronting this stage to becoming a young adult. A review of the historical legacy of adolescents' and young adults' fascination with music will be discussed to contextualize contemporary youths' fascination with rap music. Chapter 3 reviews the role and importance of parenting styles in promoting better communication with youth and why some parents may be more open to using rap music as a catalyst for conversation than others.

Chapter 4 provides an overview of the history, growth, and

development of rap music. Chapter 5 outlines the growth and development of gangsta rap and its influence on the rap community. Chapter 6 looks at the growth and development of materialistic rap and its focus on the "bling bling" of rap music. Chapter 7 looks at the history of political and protest rap and its place in the evolution of rap music. Chapter 8 reviews some of the groups and songs that are classified as "positive rap" and that promote positive messages to their listeners. Chapter 9 discusses aspects of spiritual rap and how rap has been incorporated into promoting spiritual messages. Chapter 10 briefly explains why some rap songs cannot be placed into any of the preceding categories. Chapter 11 provides an overview of the culture of hip-hop from the language and rhyme of rap to the intangible aspects of the beliefs and values of the hip-hop culture.

The psychological theories that have given rise to the spirit of rap therapy are discussed in chapter 12, and rap therapy itself is discussed in chapter 13. The following ten chapters present a variety of different case examples of rap therapy in action. The case studies illustrate the range of issues with which rap therapy can be used to assist youth and young adults in managing a variety of life's difficulties. The cases include issues ranging from behavior management difficulties, to dealing with the loss of a loved one from illness or murder. The case studies also present the use of rap therapy and rap music to improve self-esteem and manage relationship difficulties. The case studies also present the use of rap therapy in different formats from one-on-one work with different adolescents, to young men and women, to group work with adolescent boys.

The conclusion of the book is followed by a variety of appendices that can be useful for anyone wishing to gain a greater understanding of the application and function of rap therapy. I provide a list of rap songs that can be used to promote topical discussions as well as several resources that can be used to gain a better understanding of rap music and the culture of hip-hop. Several curricula that have been used in different rap therapy groups with young men, women, and children are also presented.

INTRODUCTION

I like to listen to rap music because it speaks to the lifestyle I live as a young black male. Me and my friends, other young black males love to listen to rap music. When I used to go to see white female therapists, they did not understand what could help us. They don't understand that what they are saying is going in one ear and out the other, it just gives me a headache when I go in there, I just want to get out and go get high, because it does not help me at all. . . . My reality and rap music is probably too violent for them.
—Anonymous

THE PRECEDING quote is from a 20-year-old African American male who was a patient of mine and who I'll call "Adam." Adam was mandated by the court to see a clinical psychologist for anger management training after his arrest, with two other friends, for attempted robbery. At the time of the arrest, Adam was on probation for shoplifting and possession of an illegal weapon. Adam suffered from a learning disability and had been in and out of psychotherapy for five years with several different therapists. He told me that his past treatment did not help because they (therapists) did not know what the streets were like. "I'm from the streets" is a common statement given to me by many of my inner-city clients. During our first meeting, I asked Adam what his hobbies were. He told me they included rapping and "sex with shorties from murder pan" (girls from his neighborhood). After hearing that, I began incorporating rap into our sessions.

I asked Adam who were some of his favorite artists, and he said they included Tupac and Snoop Doggy Dogg. When I asked him why he reported these artists in particular, he replied, "Because those are some real pimps, or should I say Tupac was a real pimp. I love Death Row [Records]. For them it's all about gangstas, pimps, and hoes." I asked him if he had written any raps; he said he had and proceeded to recite an original rap. The rap he recited to me was extremely angry and harsh, but incredibly creative.

After several other meetings discussing rap music and listening to his raps, I asked Adam if he thought his raps were angry. He said, "No doubt they angry. I'm an angry ass nigga; I ain't got shit to be happy about. I'm only seventeen and have already been in jail, dropped out of school, and got to deal with these dumb-ass probation officers." I challenged him to write a positive rap. He wrote about his regret and guilty feelings associated with his incarceration and parole violation. This rap provided the inroads for our ongoing discussions about his anger management difficulties as reported by the court.

Since he reported that he was a fan of the late Tupac, I challenged him to consider how Tupac's lifestyle might have contributed to his premature death. We had several discussions about how a change in lifestyle and one's thoughts about violence and being tough could potentially decrease the risk factors associated with being murdered or dealing with any other negative consequences associated with being a "gangsta." These discussions continued to evolve into conversations about how managing his anger could benefit him in multiple areas of his life, not just with the judicial system.

Adam progressively gained better control over his anger, developed alternative strategies for behaving when angry, and gained further insight into the factors that precipitated his anger. I was able to provide Adam with a greater level of insight and motivation to better manage his anger with the use of rap music than had previously been accomplished by past therapists who apparently utilized a more traditional approach with him. By incorporating rap music into our work together, Adam developed a better relationship with me and gained a greater level of ownership about his ability to better manage his anger. Rap therapy utilized some of Adam's strengths to enable him to develop the self-efficacy needed to challenge many of the self-destructive beliefs that he held close to him. Through our discussions associated with rap music and the culture of hip-hop, Adam resolved his anger management difficulties.

Although Adam's primary referral issue was due to his difficulties with managing his anger, we also further discussed his hobby of flirting and having multiple sexual partners. He initially reported that he was not concerned about safe sex and did not engage in safe-sex practices. After several more sessions discussing the value of safe sex and listening to some rap songs such as Salt 'N' Pepa's "Let's Talk about Sex" and "Toilet Tisha" by Outkast, Adam was able to begin thinking and speaking about safe sex in a new way. He was able to write a two-page rap on the risk of contracting HIV through unprotected sex. He reported that after having the discussions about safe sex, listening to rap music about safe sex, and writing raps about safe sex, he was able to change his behavior to include the use of condoms and has become more discriminating in his sexual activities. Furthermore, after incorporating rap music into our work together, he maintained all of his appointments and did not violate his parole. Through the use of rap music, Adam was able to improve his anger management difficulties, challenge his self-destructive beliefs, and gain some insight into the value of safe sex and the responsibility associated with having sex. You have just been introduced to rap therapy.

PART 1

BACKGROUND

1. YOUTH

ADOLESCENCE and entrance into early adulthood are difficult developmental stages that can have significant long-term effects on one's life. Youth attempting to navigate through this tumultuous stage are confronted with many temptations, choices, and decisions. Adolescence is marked with confronting drives about developing independence from parents. Common issues confronting youth at this stage include decisions about life, drugs, dating, sexuality, sexual behavior, risk taking, appearance, and education. The use and experimentation with alcohol, cigarettes, and drugs is common among many adolescents. The use of these substances may be due to a desire to fit in with their friends and become popular, or it may be due to rebellion or boredom. Puberty is marked by several different biological and psychological changes that contribute to greater interest in dating, intimacy, and experimentation in sexual behavior. Sex education with parental involvement can help these normal developmental curiosities be understood by reducing risky sexual behavior that can lead to unplanned pregnancy or the contraction of sexually transmitted diseases from unprotected sex. Given the broader range of independence during adolescence, many youth are confronted with greater temptations that can lead to increased risk-taking behavior. Common risky behaviors include reckless driving (which can lead to auto accidents), use of illegal drugs, and being the victim or perpetrator of violence.

Concerns about appearance also tend to become more important during adolescence. Adolescent girls are found to report lower self-esteem than boys. During adolescence, girls tend to feel less confident about school achievement and are less satisfied with their appearance. In fact, girls tend to be at the greatest risk for developing eating disorders such as anorexia nervosa and bulimia. Anorexia nervosa is a disease of intentional starvation to manage weight. Bulimia is a disorder in which one overeats and then intentionally vomits to avoid gaining weight.

Adolescents are also confronted with assessing the value they place on education. They must decide if they plan to graduate from high school, drop out of high school, go to college, or get a job.

Researchers on adolescent development such as Laurence Steinberg write and report that violent crimes and crimes against property are very high among teenagers. Furthermore, adolescents have a high incidence of being victims of violent crimes. As the Centers for Disease Control (CDC) reports, homicide is the second leading cause of death for youth between the ages of ten and nineteen. Furthermore, homicide is the leading cause of death among African Americans between the ages of fifteen and twenty-four and the second leading cause of death for Hispanic youth. The CDC reports that the following list of risk factors for youth violence are significant and should be taken seriously by parents and care givers:

Beliefs that support violent behavior
Antisocial behavior

Bullying other children
Criminal behavior
Use of alcohol
Parental drug use
Poor parental supervision
Exposure to violence
Antisocial parents
Socializing with peers with antisocial behavior
Low commitment to school
Access to firearms

Given all these challenges, adolescents are also found to be at a greater risk for attempting and committing suicide. The CDC reports that 15 percent of all suicides committed in 2000 were among people under the age of twenty-five. The CDC also reports that from 1980 to 1997 the rate of suicide increased 109 percent for persons between the ages of ten and fourteen and from 1980 to 1996 the rate increased 105 percent for African American males aged fifteen to nineteen. The suicide rate among young people is greatest for white males; however, from 1980 to 1995 the suicide rates increased most rapidly among young African American males. As reported by the *World Book*, four factors are found to place adolescents at risk for suicidal behavior: (1) stress from school or relationships, (2) low self-esteem or depression, (3) family conflict, and (4) having a history of suicidal behavior in the family.

The challenge and stress associated with the multiple decisions of this developmental stage can intensify the negative influence of any preexisting risk factors. Common environmental risk factors that are linked to risky decision making include:

Poverty
Poor relationships with parents

Overcrowded housing conditions
Child abuse
Exposure to frequent acts of violence
Poor school performance
Parents with mental health challenges
Parents with histories of involvement with the criminal jus-
tice system

Adam's case is a good example of how risk factors can be intensified during adolescent decision making. Two of Adam's risk
factors included poverty and poor academic performance in
school. He also glorified the antisocial lyrics of many rap songs,
which reinforced his risky decision-making process. Each of these
factors was found to contribute to his decisions about shoplifting
and dropping out of school. Adam's experience is not an unusual
one for many urban youth who are the victims of multiple risk
factors and limited access to support systems that can help them
overcome these risk factors or gain insight into how to manage
them effectively.

My experiences working in an inner-city public hospital, an
inner-city community health center, and inner-city public schools
in Boston and Chicago have in many ways presented very common themes, diagnoses, and stories. One common experience
people share with me in these settings is their exposure to several
different forms of psychological trauma. Severe trauma often manifests symptomatically as post-traumatic stress disorder (PTSD).

PTSD is a psychological disorder associated with serious trau-
matic events. Common symptoms of PTSD include intrusive
memories of the trauma, nightmares of the trauma, avoidance of
the trauma, numbness from the trauma, and hypervigilance in
settings that may cause further trauma. Trauma is manifested
through traditional and nontraditional forms. Some common tra-

ditional forms of trauma include witnessing murder, physical abuse, sexual abuse, and emotional abuse through abandonment. Common nontraditional forms of trauma frequently seen in inner-city clinical settings include chronic institutional racism, poverty, unemployment, homelessness, and generational cycles of poor academic performance.

In addition to experiencing trauma or being raised by parents who are trauma survivors, many youth also have difficulties with attention, concentration, depression, and behavior in school and home. I recently conducted a survey to determine what middle school children perceive as the most stressful and anxiety-provoking issues confronting them at school. The survey was done with a multicultural group of 765 middle school children. The results of the survey find that the presence and use of drugs and alcohol are the most stressful issues confronting these children. The latter is not surprising considering the prevalence of substance abuse problems reported by the Center on Addiction and Substance Abuse (CASA). CASA reports that more than 70 percent of fifteen to seventeen year olds report that drugs are used, sold, and kept at their schools. The survey I conducted also finds that peer pressure is another issue considered by adolescent youth to be very stressful. If my findings can be generalized and considered to be common issues confronting youth, then interventions with youth must acknowledge the prevalence and influence of trauma, peer pressure, and drugs on the development of youth and young adults. Interestingly, these are also common themes discussed in music listened to by youth.

2. YOUTH AND MUSIC

Each generation of youth has had a special connection to music. The belief that music speaks to their experiences, challenges, passions, fears, and hopes is in many ways the cornerstone of being an adolescent or young adult. Different forms of music have spoken to youth over time. Music enjoyed by youth has historically been radical and in opposition to adult values and norms. The defiant musical interest of youth can easily be traced back to the beginning of rock 'n' roll in the 1950s with such artists as Chuck Berry ("Johnny B. Goode"), Little Richard ("Good Golly Miss Molly"), Sam Cooke ("You Send Me"), and Elvis Presley, who the *Columbia Encyclopedia* describes as "horrifying" older people (parents).

Youth have also had a long history of gravitating to "protest" music such as Bob Dylan's "Blowin' in the Wind." During the Vietnam War, protest music evolved to include commentary on topics such as sex, war, and drugs. Groups such as Jefferson Airplane, the Grateful Dead, and the Beatles were arguably the most popular groups among youth during this time period. Furthermore, concerts given by many of these historic rock 'n' roll artists included extensive drug use (e.g., Woodstock in 1969) and occasional fatal violent outbursts such as during the Rolling Stones' 1969 concert in Altamont, California. Many of these historic music icons sang of drugs and encouraged drug use among the youthful audience at their concerts. Several of the artists who popularized drug use such as Janis Joplin, Jim Morrison, and Jimi Hendrix eventually died of overdose. Interestingly, these deaths did not decrease the amount of drug use by their audience.

In the 1970s, rock 'n' roll evolved into "punk rock" and became much more violent in its lyrics and stage presence, while the messages of political protest remained central. Many American youth were seduced and influenced by the lyrics of such groups as the Clash and Sex Pistols, which paved the way for the next generation, who adored such groups as Nirvana and Pearl Jam.

Reggae has also had a significant influence on the global music scene. Many argue that reggae has influenced soul, rhythm and blues, and rock music, while others suggest that reggae was influenced by rhythm and blues and soul music. Regardless of the source of the direction of influence, reggae has had and continues to have a significant influence on many youth. Reggae's songs of protest, liberation, and freedom have been celebrated and sung all over the world. Reggae began to gain popularity outside Jamaica in the late 1960s through the recordings of a number of reggae artists. The most influential was Bob Marley, who grew up in Kingston, Jamaica. For many youth around the world in the '70s and '80s, Bob Marley represented a music icon that idealized the potential of music contributing to several different international political agendas. Marley's songs of political protest include "Exodus," "Zimbabwe," "Rebel Music," and "Stir It Up." He also wrote "I Shot the Sheriff," which became a hit in a recording by Eric Clapton in 1974. As with many other forms of music enjoyed by youth, reggae also had a significant drug culture spearheaded by the use of marijuana.

Shows such as *Behind the Music* on VH-1 and other weekly entertainment shows on network television have done a good job revealing the detrimental effects of drugs on many historic and contemporary music icons, but they have not decreased the amount of drug consumption by their listeners. While rock and punk music continue to exist, their mass appeal has recently been eclipsed by rap music, the new music of choice for many youth today. Like its predecessors, rap music discusses all the social ills of our society and is the victim of the same criticisms.

In many ways, the music that youth listened to prior to 1980 was regional and influenced by what was played on local radio. However, with the advent of syndicated television, cable television, satellite television, syndicated radio, online radio, satellite radio, the Internet, and music sharing online through MP3 and Web sites, the music youth listen to and identify with is no longer simply regional. Technology has opened a new door to music consumption that is now global. Rap music in many ways has developed, evolved, and grown in parallel with many of these technological advancements. Today, most urban and suburban youth listen to rap music and are influenced by the lyrics of rap music on an international level.

A recent comment by an eighteen-year-old client that I am working with in therapy underscores this point. He told me, "I began using drugs because I loved the *Chronic* [a CD by Dr. Dre] and I wanted to see what it would be like to use chronic." This young man is now in treatment at a residential substance abuse treatment program. He goes on to report that he is "happy that we use rap music in our therapeutic work together, because rap music got me here and it only makes sense that rap music will get me back on track, 'cause you know I'm a hip-hop head for life." This commentary is far too common with the youth and young adults that I work with and have helped in the past. If you listen to the colloquial sayings that are common among many youth, these sayings have come from rap songs, videos, or hip-hop movies. Many youth are oblivious to the influence that rap music has had on their communication, vocabulary, thoughts, beliefs, behaviors, and actions.

Interestingly, many of the same issues reported by adolescents to be incredibly stressful are common themes discussed in rap songs. This has been true since the inception of rap music, when it primarily spoke of the challenges of growing up. In 1982, the Furious Five released a legendary rap song titled "The Message," in which they vividly describe the difficulties of growing up in their community as young adults: "It's like a jungle sometimes it makes me wonder, how I keep from going under." Other historic rap music icons such as Curtis Blow, Whodini, Run DMC, Doug E. Fresh, Slick Rick, Boggie Down Productions, MC Lyte, and Salt 'N' Pepa also spoke of the difficulties of growing up in the inner city. In 1993, Tupac suggested "keep ya head up" while dealing with the complexities and realities confronted by young women challenged with the stress of sexism and transitions into womanhood. The angst of this developmental stage discussed by rappers is not exclusive to inner-city black rappers, but is also discussed by white rappers. The latter date back to 1980 with Blondie and 1982 with the Beastie Boys' debut. More recently, white strife is heard through the music of Eminem, Kid Rock, and Limp Bizkit.

Latino influences on rap music and the culture of hip-hop date back to the inception of the culture with the Rock Steady Crew and other break dancers and graffiti artists. In the early stages of the advent of rap music, Latino rappers did not get much time on the microphone; however, Latino rappers such as the Late Big Pun, Beatnuts and Fat Joe, The Terror Squad, and Cuban Link are getting a lot of airplay now and are using rap to convey, inform, and speak of issues from a Latin perspective. As with all forms of rap music, Latin rap has its critics such as Gabe Morales, a gang specialist for King County Correctional Facility who discusses and writes about the many gangs in California rallying around violent themes in certain Latino rap songs to promote greater violence and recruit more Latino gang members. In particular, he mentions a rap group known as Darkroom Familia, who recently released a rap CD entitled *Gang Stories*. A section of the CD liner from *Gang Stories* reads: "We live la vida loca. Violence solves everything!" However, Latino rap, like all other forms of rap, is a mixed bag: there is the good, the bad, and the ugly, and just about all of rap music can be used for educational purposes.

Furthermore, European, Asian, African, Australian, and South American rappers are currently representing the international appeal and identification rap music has had on the global stage. The diverse cultural background of rappers singing about common challenges speaks to the generality of these issues during the stages of preadolescence, adolescence, and early adult development. The similarities between the concerns, strife, and stressors of youth and rap music are reportedly due to rap music being based on the reality of many young rappers' lives. Speaking of rap music, in the words of GuRu on his CD *Jazzmatazz:*

It is musical cultural expression based on reality.

3. PARENTING STYLES

RAP THERAPY is most influential when viewed as a means of using rap music to communicate and teach youth who enjoy listening to rap music and are influenced by rap music lyrics and culture. Many parents view rap music as a tool they can use to improve communication with their child, while others not only do not discuss themes in their child's favorite music, but may even forbid their child to listen to rap music. Each parent has different parenting styles, which influences his or her communication with his or her child.

Developmental psychologists find that parents tend to have very distinct and different ways of communicating with their children depending on the parenting style they use. Certain parenting styles are known to facilitate better communication between child and parent than others. Diana Baumrind's theory of parenting styles is a relevant issue to consider when parents attempt to improve communication with their children. Baumrind breaks parenting styles down into three predominant categories: permissive, authoritarian, and authoritative. Other researchers also speak of a fourth parenting style known as uninvolved.

The permissive parenting style is one in which the parents are

19

warm, accepting, and encouraging of their child's creativity. They often accept and affirm their child's impulses and desires. This parenting style involves ongoing consultation with the child and provides expectations around family rules. This parenting style makes few demands on having the child behave in a mature manner. Researchers find that children raised by parents using a permissive parenting style often have difficulty controlling their impulses and taking responsibility for their actions and are generally immature.

The authoritarian parenting style is one in which the parents are highly controlling in their use of authority and usually enforce their rule through punishment. They expect obedience from their child and do not expect disagreement or resistance to their wishes. They shape and control the behavior of their child by following a predetermined theoretical framework of how parenting is "supposed" to be done. This parenting style is often described by the child as one in which his or her parents believe "that children were meant to be seen not heard." Researchers find that children raised by authoritarian parents tend to have difficulties developing social competence, have lower self-esteem, and have difficulty with taking the initiative on projects.

The authoritative parenting style encourages give and take in communication. The parents inform their child of the reasons for their decisions and expectations. The parents are strong when it is necessary to be strong with discipline and compassionate when necessary. These parents recognize what their interests are and also acknowledge the child's own individual strengths and characteristics. They accept the child's current attributes and strengths and like authoritarian parents they set goals for their child's future development. However, unlike authoritarian parents who do not allow much freedom in the expectations they set forth for their child, authoritative parents allow their child enough freedom of expression in accomplishing goals that the child develops greater independence and autonomy. Research findings concerning children raised by authoritative parents suggest that they are the best-adjusted children in terms of social competence.

The uninvolved parenting style is one in which the parents do not demand much of their child and do not expect much. They are indifferent to their child's accomplishments and may not have many goals for him or her. The extreme of the uninvolved parenting style is one of neglect and/or abandonment. Children raised by parents using an uninvolved parenting style may be at a greater risk of developing difficulty managing their impulses and learning the give-and-take aspects of interpersonal relationships.

Each of these four parenting styles can be thought of as different ways in which parents communicate with their children. Authoritative parents utilize a child's interest in rap music as a tool for teaching their child about the content of the music or why they do not think that certain songs are healthy to listen to. Authoritarian parents simply forbid their child from listening to rap music without any explanation and may punish their child if they find out that the child has been listening to rap music. Permissive parents allow their child to listen to rap music if the child chooses to do so but do not necessarily use the opportunity to teach the child about the content of the lyrics or any other educational aspect of listening to this type of music. Uninvolved parents allow their child to listen to any type of music he or she wants to listen to without any concern or interest in their child's desire to listen to music at all.

Parenting styles of communication do not occur in a vacuum. Parenting styles and forms of communication are a dynamic process that occurs in relation to the personality of the child. Children have preferred ways of responding to stimuli and parental styles. These preferential responses are known as temperaments.

Some children have oppositional temperaments, while others have easy-going and accepting temperaments. Developmental psychologists cluster children's temperaments into three broad categories: an easy temperament, a difficult temperament, and a slow-to-warm-up temperament. Children with an easy temperament tend to be happy, calm, adaptable, and a bit easier to manage in comparison to the other two temperament styles. Children that have a difficult temperament style are easily frustrated and upset, are fussy, and may be a bit higher strung in their interactions with others. Children with a slow-to-warm-up temperament are also fussy like the difficult children, but it is because they may be a bit more shy and timid and have difficulty adjusting to new situations. However, they eventually warm up and develop relationships that are more agreeable.

Given the different parental styles and different temperaments of children, it is important that parents attempt to modify their parenting style to support and fit their child's temperamental predisposition. In other words, it is the goodness of fit between the parents' parenting style and the temperament of the child.

In general, several points are helpful for parents to be aware of as they attempt to improve communication with their child. Parents should keep in mind the importance and value of supportive communication. It is always helpful to listen to a child's perspective and encourage him or her to have his or her own view on matters. It is helpful to have the child be involved in finding solutions to problems when appropriate. Communication with a child is improved when parents explain the expectations they have for their child and remain steadfast in the decisions they make. It is also important for parents to know what their child's interests and strengths are and attempt to improve communication with their child by focusing on the child's strengths, not his or her limitations or weaknesses. Parents can improve communication with their child by recognizing what their child's interests are and developing strategies to utilize those issues that their child is most interested in and as a common ground for facilitating better communication, education, and relationship building. This is what rap therapy is all about: utilizing a child's interest in rap music to communicate important lessons in life. Rather than forbid a child to listen to rap music because it is too violent, which will oftentimes promote rebellion in the child, use the violent lyrics in the song to discuss why violence is bad, discuss why the rapper sings of violent themes, and so on. Utilizing a child's interest in rap music as a focal point for improving communication, understanding, education, and relationship building is the goal of rap therapy.

4. RAP MUSIC

RAP MUSIC is different from hip-hop. Rap is the music, the beats, and the rhyme of a culture known as hip-hop. As will be discussed in greater detail in the pages to come, rap music is simply a part of the broader culture of hip-hop. Rap music is said to have its genesis in the early 1970s in the Bronx. Since then, it has grown into a billion-dollar global industry that has taken on the identity of a cultural movement. Rap music has grown from an idiosyncratic form of expression in the ghettos of New York City to the topic of conversation for many cultural critics and the theme of global conferences. The subject of rap and hip-hop has also recently become the guest at the ivory tower of American academia, such as the Hip-Hop Conference at the University of Michigan in the spring of 2001 and Cornel West's reflections about hip-hop that were presented at the Harvard School of Government in October 2001. Furthermore, hip–hop has become the subject matter for college courses such as "Hip-Hop Nation: Pop Culture and Urban Youth," which is taught at DePaul University in Chicago.

Rap music has not only become popular with youth and intellectuals doing research, but it has also captured the attention and fondness of many urban adults. The other day I was driving with my mother and listening to V-103 in Chicago. V-103 typically has a music format of rhythm and blues (R&B) from the 1970s through the 1990s. However, on this particular day it was featuring "Big Mama" by LL Cool J on his new CD *10*. The song is dedicated to his grandmother. For the next two hours, the forty- to fifty-year-old crowd of listeners were calling in to praise the song. Most comments went something like this: "Man, I don't normally listen to rap music, but that song is the bomb, if you don't like that song you ain't got no soul," or "Oh my goodness, that song reminds me of my grandmother and all the things we did together forty-five years ago, hope you play more music like that." Rap music is not only influential on youth, but it also continues to influence adults, educators, clergy, public health, and many other global communities.

Rap music grew out of the interaction of poverty, music, dance, graffiti, and fun. Historical icons that contributed to the birth of rap music include DJ Kool Herc, Afrika Bambaataa, Grandmaster Flash, Soul Sonic Force, the Cold Crush Brothers, and the Sugar Hill Gang. The Sugar Hill Gang's smash hit "Rapper's Delight" was the first rap song to climb the Billboard R & B charts to number 4 in the fall of 1979. In 1982, the release of "The Message" by Grandmaster Flash and the Furious Five marked the beginning of another major milestone in the growth and development of rap music. "The Message" marked a turn in rap music from simply being music about fun and dance to presenting a commentary on the anger, politics, issues, and challenges confronting black adolescents and young adults.

In the early to mid-1980s, rap music took another step forward in its evolution with the introduction of new artists such as Kurtis Blow, Whodini, Run DMC, the Fat Boys, LL Cool J, and Eric B and Rakim to name a few. New record labels such as Def Jam, Death Row, Profile, and Tommy Boy also began to spawn.

The mid '80s also marked the beginning of rap music's significant national influence on music, art, media, and the social development of youth.

With this in mind, children born in 1985 and later can be considered the offspring of the rap and hip-hop era. As Nelson George suggests in his 1998 book *Hip Hop America,* rap music has influenced a variety of socialization processes of urban youth of color, ranging from clothing to language. Master P's success as a rap artist is a fine example of the insatiable consumption of rap stimuli by today's youth. Master P's self-promoted movie *I'm Bout It* (1997) never made it to commercial theaters, but it was a home video blockbuster that topped music video sales and competed with *Jerry Maguire* (1996) for top spots on Billboard's video scan chart.

Rap music has also been the subject of considerable political debate. In 1992, Ice T's song "Cop Killer" was blamed by many police officers for inciting and causing the Los Angeles riots that took place in 1992. Furthermore, the Combined Law Enforcement Agency of Texas led a national boycott against Time Warner, who owned the rights to Ice T's song. The boycott became so influential that President George Bush, Vice President Dan Quayle, and National Security Council Aid Oliver North each spoke publicly on national television about the detrimental influence of "Cop Killer," specifically, and rap music, in general, on youth. Since 1992, many religious leaders throughout the country have led local and national campaigns about the negative influence of rap music. However, many of these efforts have simply increased the demand for rap music and products. Some religious leaders have recognized the potential utility of rap music to convey positive messages to youth. Rap music has recently been incorporated into gospel music and sermons to convey a religious message to those who may otherwise not listen to spiritual messages.

These political and religious controversies concerning the influence of rap music personify the national impact that rap music has had on American society and politics for the past two decades. Rap music has become such a large industry that it is now the subject of national summit meetings, multiple award shows, and international magazines. Rap music has also recently been used by Fortune 500 companies, public health organizations, sports teams, and the media to market products to urban youth. Rap music's influence on people and society is undeniably significant.

Rap music can be categorized into six general categories: (1) gangsta rap, (2) materialistic rap, (3) political/protest rap, (4) positive rap, (5) spiritual rap, and (6) rap not otherwise specified, which includes music with rap fusion. However, most rappers' artistic expression crosses several, if not all, categories. Rap music is very complex and diverse, given the multiple genres that comprise it. The genres of rap are not simply based on geography or a particular time in rap history, but also on personality and sociology. Personality of the artists as individuals and the group they belong to as a collective contributes to their artistic expression in many ways. Furthermore, the social conditions in which they developed as a group have a significant influence on their particular identification with rap music. With this in mind, the next six chapters review the different categories of rap music.

5. GANGSTA RAP

The boyz n the hood are always hard.
—*Boyz N the Hood*

GANGSTA (gangster) rap is personified by the music of rap groups such as Niggaz with Attitude and Above the Law and music produced by Death Row Records (now The Row) and Master P's "No Limit." It can be said to focus on violence, guns, misogyny, and profane language. Gangsta rap promotes an antisocial message of violence, crime, and sexism.

The origins of gangsta rap come primarily from resource-poor communities that are confronted with a number of issues that are not endured by economically stable communities. This continues to be the case for many young rappers who see hip-hop as a means to an end of the poverty in which they grew up. Most notably, poor communities are plagued by higher violence, crime, and mortality rates. These higher rates of violence contribute to reduced life expectancies, which creates a very different meaning of adolescence for many of those rappers who come from these poor communities.

As a consequence of living in these community settings, many young rappers perceive adolescence as a shortened period and are driven to enter adulthood at a faster rate. For many, there is a sense of urgency to engage in what they consider to be "grownup" activities because of the higher incidence of deaths and incarceration seen within their communities.

With this in mind, it is not surprising that many of the gangsta rappers sing of these themes and glorify these images in their rap videos. This is the very argument that many of the gangsta rap artists use when they suggest that their music simply reflects the reality of the circumstances they witnessed growing up or continue to witness in their communities. Furthermore, they argue that their music is a broadcast to the world of the misery and inhumane circumstances that many people living in urban poor ghetto communities must confront on a daily basis. They suggest that they are simply the reporters of the atrocities of the inner city and that their commentaries share the psychology and orientation of many of the people who live the lifestyle about which they rap.

In Los Angeles (LA) rap music was the beat on the streets in the early 1980's as conflict between the Crips and Bloods (LA street gangs) intensified with the increasing presence of cocaine and other drugs. Graffiti artists depicting violence became the artistic backdrop to the economic and judicial misery of many of the West Coast communities. These are some of the factors that gave rise to the subject content for many of the burgeoning rappers from the West Coast. Easy E, Ice Cube, Dr. Dre, MC Ren, and DJ Yella formed Niggaz with Attitude (NWA), one of the most well-known early gangsta rap groups from southcentral LA. NWA was one of the first rap groups to push the envelope by publicly discussing the mind-set of gangstas in their music. Dr. Dre and other members of NWA wanted to make hit records that reflected what was going on in their neighborhood.

Prior to gangsta rap taking off in southcentral LA, gangsta lyrics were being developed and presented in New York and Philadelphia. Schoolly D's "PSK—What Does It Mean" is considered to be one of the first gangsta rap songs. The song is about a stick-up kid who is a member of the Parkside Killers. Boogie Down Productions, which was composed of KRS-1 and Scott La Rock, made "Criminal Minded," which many argue was the beginning of gangsta rap in New York City. However, neither Schoolly D nor Boogie Down Productions made lyrics that glorified violence to the degree of NWA or other West Coast rappers.

In the 1990s, gangsta rap garnered greater mainstream attention with Ice T's song "Cop Killer." Not only did "Cop Killer" get wide-spread attention due to the content of the song, but it also bridged gangsta rap lyrics with rock music, which generated a broad cross section of attention. As "Cop Killer" glorified violence against police, other factors took place in the '90s that increased the general paranoia of many American police departments. The Rodney King beating in LA generated greater national concern about police brutality, which in turn converted many more sympathetic ears to the mantras of the gangsta rap movement. The beliefs of many urban residents was best spoken by Ice Cube (with NWA) in the song "Fuck the Police," in which he suggests that because he is a person of color with some jewelry or a pager the police may be out to arrest him or worst yet, to kill him. As Ice Cube raps about the police, he says that they

think they have the authority to kill a minority.

As reports of police brutality continued to get mainstream attention on the news, more and more rappers sang about the injustices and hypocrisy of the American legal and judicial system, which gave gangsta rap a political agenda. However, as gangsta rap transitioned from the late 1980s to the 1990s, the early political agenda of gangsta rap was quickly overlooked by many young naive rappers who only took notice of the violent themes of the music. These new rappers contributed to a growing number of gangsta rap songs that simply glorified the violence and aggression of gangsta rap.

The 1990s also saw the growth of Suge Knight and Death Row Records. Suge Knight is said to have run Death Row Records just like a gangsta mob boss. He reportedly was able to get Death Row Records to release Dr. Dre from his contract with NWA by threatening Easy E. Likewise, it is reported that he was able to have several rappers sign over the rights of their music through threats and intimidation. Gangsta rap had now transitioned from creative stories of the activities of the ghetto to becoming a real management style and behavior. Death Row Records' gangsta rap mentality eventuality contributed to its downfall. Suge Knight was put on probation after beating two rappers. Dr. Dre was put on house arrest for breaking someone's jaw and Snoop Doggy Dogg was in court for charges of being an accessory to murder after his bodyguard shot a gang member. Death Row Records eventually signed the late Tupac Shakur, who fit the rough and hard gangsta rap presentation well. Although Tupac also rapped about things other than guns, violence, and being a gangsta, when he signed with Death Row he exaggerated his hard persona.

During the 1990s, several "hard" and gangsta East Coast rappers began to rap about guns, violence, and antisocial behavior as well. The late Notorious B.I.G., Mobb Deep, the Lost Boyz, and other East Coast rappers began rapping about being gangstas. The glorification of gangsta rap content has become the norm for many rap artists now. As rappers such as the late Tupac and 50 Cents glorify the fact that they have been shot several times and survived to sing about it, they convey a message to young impressionable listeners that living the thug life will not necessarily lead to death. Unfortunately, many youth believe these messages and begin to glorify and value these rites of passage into becoming a thug or gangsta. They begin to believe that they are not hard, tough, or worthy of respect if they have not been the victims of a shooting, drive by, or stick up. Rap therapy attempts to challenge and restructure these delusional masochistic beliefs. In fact, these themes can be discussed with many youth to help them begin to realize the dangers of living the gangsta rapper lifestyle or the so-called thug life.

The opponents of gangsta rap argue that the music simply glorifies and endorses crime and violence. Furthermore, they suggest that while the music may be a reflection of the dark realities of the inner city, it does more than simply expose this message to the general public: it also reinforces and glorifies the violence and crime of the inner city. Many suggest that the phrase "ghetto fabulous" was born in part by gangsta rap music's glorification and reinforcement of the worst aspects of the lifestyles of the poor inner-city communities in America. Others suggest that by glorifying the lifestyle of the inner-city gangstas, gangsta rap not only reinforces their behavior, but also encourages and promotes this lifestyle to the millions of impressionable children and young adults who listen to the lyrics of gangsta music. In doing so, the music is said to reinforce and generalize racist stereotypes that contribute to the difficulties these communities have had in overcoming the obstacles of poor education, unemployment, and violence that have plagued them for years.

In the late 1980s and early 1990s, during gangsta rap's height, many young white youth began calling themselves "niggas" and the culture of gangsta rap spread throughout the world. Several reporters covering the war on terrorism in Afghanistan write about the spread of gangsta rap. More specifically, they report on how several members of the Taliban could be seen driving through Kabul with "tricked out low rider pick up trucks reciting lyrics from Dr. Dre and Snoop Doggy Dogg from their *Chronic* CD."

6. MATERIALISTIC RAP

As put by *The Vibe History of Hip Hop*, the materialism of rap has become fine jewelry and "designer clothing, imported champagne, Cuban cigars, [and] luxury automobiles." Materialistic rap, unlike gangsta rap, focuses on promoting messages of the value of wealth, sex, possessions, and the trappings of affluence. "HarlemWorld" by Mase, "Spend a Little Doe" by Lil' Kim, and "Forever" by Puff Daddy personify materialistic rap. Each of these songs glorifies the "bling bling" that has come to be known as the foundation of rap music's capitalistic vision. Materialistic rap does not necessarily discuss a strategy to obtain wealth, however, it focuses on the lifestyle that wealth can provide. Songs such as the Big Tymers's "Hood Rich" personify the focus of materialism without employment as they proudly proclaim:

Ain't got no job but I stay fly.

The music videos and lyrics of these songs often make reference to expensive jewelry, clothing, food, spirits, extravagant parties, vacations or travels to exotic locations, exclusive automobiles and homes, cruising yachts, and/or private jets. In many ways, materialistic rap can be conceptualized as the soap opera of rap music. Materialistic and gangsta rap together are what have given rise to the concept of "ghetto fabulous." While gangsta rap glorifies certain aspects of the thug mentality of the ghetto, materialistic rap has made certain aspects of the ghetto lifestyle exclusive, desirable, and associated with wealth. This "bling bling" of rap music is reinforced by the celebrity status of rap stars.

Materialistic rap is a perfect fit for the orientation of American capitalism and America has capitalized on the presence of rap music. Rap music has become one of the most influential tools for marketing products to American youth and urban adults. Rap artists are seen and heard daily on a variety of commercials singing jingles and promoting the materialism of their image. Rap music's commercial influence is even seen in its presence in video games marketed to a large cross section of society.

With this in mind, materialistic rap has become rap music's "pop" music. It is verbally digestible with fewer uses of profane language than gangsta rap. It exemplifies the brighter side of rap music by endorsing consumption as opposed to violence, which is a bit easier to consume by mainstream America. The motto of materialistic rap, as coined by P Diddy, is "it's all about the benjamins" (short for $100 bills).

As rap music progressively became mainstream and its popularity began to cross socioeconomic and cultural barriers, its appeal and importance to record executives became more apparent. Rappers where not just singing about making money, they were actually being paid big money by top recording labels. Rap music had entered its adulthood when it began being mass marketed through different mediums. The materialism of rap music was not only seen in the clothing, jewelry, and cars driven by rap superstars, but also through the mass marketing in movies, videos, and new clothing lines. The progressive development of materialistic rap coincided with rap music's enormous commercial and economic contribution to the American economy. As Nelson George discusses in *Hip Hop America,* rap magazines such as *Source, Vibe,* and *XXL* are as much about advertising and marketing for these economies with interdependent relationships with hip-hop as they are about writing about rap music. Designers such as Ralph Lauren, Calvin Klein, Channel, and other designers utilize the influence of rap music to further market their products. Furthermore, the advent of hip-hop's own clothing lines such as Phat Pharm, Mecca USA, FUBU, Ecko, Lugz, and others has propelled the self-sufficient marketability of rap to a higher level. Rap music has become a billion-dollar industry and as such it has developed its own cultural identity. Terms such as "ghetto fabulous" personify and demonstrate hip-hop's insatiable appetite and consumption of Prada, Armani, Dolce and Gabbana, expensive real estate, and cars. In his 1997 book *Fight the Power,* Chuck D suggests that one of the conscious and unconscious messages conveyed to many youth who are products of the hip-hop culture is that if you are not a professional athlete, entertainer, or "living a lavish lifestyle then you ain't shit."

Materialistic rap proves that nobody likes being poor; even those who glorify the philosophical assets of poverty like to "bling bling" every now and then. However, given materialistic rap's widespread appeal and consumption, it could serve a greater educational role by occasionally educating its listeners about strategies for gaining wealth. Most, if not all, of the rappers that have become successful have worked very hard for their success. They have tirelessly sacrificed for their art. These messages need to be conveyed to those who learn from their lyrics. Some of the newer shows on MTV that give a glimpse into the hard work of becoming a rap performer are beneficial, in that they educate youth about the perseverance and sacrifice that contribute to success. It is believed that these lessons could be generalized to other areas of growth and development that require patience, perseverance, commitment, and practice for success, such as education, entrepreneurship, or promotion within one place of employment.

7. POLITICAL/PROTEST RAP

THE power of rap music to be a political voice for people oppressed throughout the world is best summed up by Chuck D writing about an experience during a Public Enemy European tour in which a Croatian fan informed him how influential Public Enemy was on many of his political beliefs. The fan reported that it was because of Public Enemy's music that he learned how to use music to express his attitudes and political beliefs of promoting peace and understanding to his countrymen and women about the religious wars between Bosnia, Herzegovina, and Croatia.

Political/protest rap developed out of the music of Gil Scott Heron and the Last Poets. It is rap music that has a political message or takes a political stand. It is best illustrated by the music of Public Enemy, KRS-1, Sister Souljah, and X-Clan. It focuses on political issues, racism, sexism, equality, and ethnic identity. For example, KRS-1's "Stop the Violence" is a rap classic that promoted the value of violence prevention. Political rap is known to take on big political issues such as drugs, sexism, racism, the judicial system, poverty, and apartheid and bring them to public attention during periods of entertainment. Chuck D is reported to have said that the goal of Public Enemy was to "uplift black youth" to believing they can make a difference politically. Public Enemy was actively involved in the Rock the Vote campaign promoted by MTV to get youth involved in politics by voicing their political positions through voting. Chuck D is also known to have referred to rap music as the CNN of the black community because of the political messages conveyed by rap music. However, he reportedly changed his opinion after the onslaught of decadent meaningless rap became popular and referred to rap music as the cartoon network of the black community. Chuck D remains a political force in the rap industry.

Political rap was a bit more prevalent in the early days of rap music. It has since taken a constant decline in popularity. However, some contemporary artists such as Dead Prez, Lauryn Hill, Wyclef Jean, and others continue to carry political messages in their music. Mos Def's commentary on America's fascination with purchasing bottled water or Queen Latifah's U.N.I.T.Y. are good examples of the contemporary political commentary of rap music. Salt 'N' Pepa's "Let's Talk about Sex" and the public service announcement they did on their *Very Necessary* CD with *We Talk* titled "I've Got Aids" is another example of the use of rap music to promote a political message. Another example of the easily forgotten political history of rap music and rap artists includes "Self Destruction," in which a group of rappers—KRS-1, MCDelight of Stetsasonic, Kool Moe Dee, MC Lyte, Just Ice, Doug E. Fresh, Heavy D, and Public Enemy—worked together on this song to promote a message of "violence prevention."

The culture of hip-hop also has a history of making significant contributions back to the community as a means of having a political voice. Sister Souljah's 1990 proposal of having a rap concert at the Apollo Theater to raise proceeds to fund a summer camp for underprivileged inner-city youth demonstrates the political good of rap music. The 1990 concert featured Public Enemy, Heavy D, Big Daddy Kane, LL Cool J, MC Lyte, and Stetsasonic and raised over $60,000 to open the African Youth Survival Camp. Sister Souljah has since worked as a director for a similar camp sponsored by P Diddy known as Daddy's House.

Political rap demonstrates the value of rap music as an educational tool, since it can educate many people about issues that they may never have been exposed to or thought about in depth. It is not uncommon to hear people who have been listening to rap music speak about how rap music has changed and is not as "political" or "educational" as it once was. Basically, these people are indicating that rap music played a significant role in their lives and that they have learned from the music that they once sang to naively. The same argument holds true for the negative impact that gangsta rap can have on influencing how one views life or has interactions with others. This subliminal influence of music must be considered as a relevant sociological tool for teaching positive messages about life. Contemporary artists that have several political messages in their music include Lauryn Hill and Wyclef Jean. On his CD *Masquerade,* Wyclef raps about peace in "War No More":

Let me hear the Middle East say peace.

Political rap, unlike gangsta rap and materialistic rap, is not as popular to audiences or producers unless it is making a political commentary about itself. As Wyclef Jean does on his CD *Masquerade,* he speaks of all the fake gangstas in hip-hop portraying themselves like they are real thugs in "You Say Keep It Gangsta":

Stop with the posing, ya'll ain't really holding.

An example of a rap about the internal politics of rap music is Common's rap "I Used to Love Her," in which he speaks about many of the growing pains of rap music, as it transitioned itself from the type of themes that were more prevalent during its youth, such as self-respect, politics, and self-love, to some of the more common themes heard in commercial rap music today, such as drugs, violence, materialistic consumption, and sexism. Other contemporary aspects of the politics of rap music include Russell Simmons's (the CEO of Def Jam Records) organization of the Hip-Hop Summit, in which rap artists, producers, music executives, academics, and social critics gather annually to brainstorm and discuss strategies for rap music to serve as a vehicle for education, political awareness, and activism.

It is unfortunate that political/protest rap has declined in popularity given that it has a significant place in the history, growth, and development of rap music. Furthermore, it has been found to have a significant positive influence on many youth who listened to the lyrics. This was seen by the Stop the Violence movement that took place in the 1980s following the release of Boogie Down Productions' *By All Means Necessary* CD. The Stop the Violence movement was spearheaded by KRS-1, who did a forty-city college tour and reportedly raised over $400,000 to help the Urban League fight violence in the inner city. The theme song for the movement was "Self Destruction," in which an all-star cast of rappers such as Chuck D, Kool Moe Dee, MC Lyte, and others promoted the values of putting an end to the senseless killings taking place in many inner-city settings.

Political rap, like positive rap and spiritual rap, is limited in its commercial distribution in comparison to gangsta and materialistic rap. Several artists listed as positive rappers can also be considered as promoting political messages, such as the Roots' recent collaboration with People for the Ethical Treatment of Animals stemming from their vegetarian lifestyle. Other contemporary artists that bridge political and positive rap are Talib Kweli, Common, and Mos Def.

8. POSITIVE RAP

I know I can be what I want to be.
—Nas, "I Can" *(God's Son)*

POSITIVE RAP, like political rap, is oftentimes not as commercial as gangsta or materialistic rap. Positive rap by rap artists such as De La Soul, A Tribe Called Quest, Nas, Common, Wyclef Jean, and Talib Kweli promote the values of education, responsibility, and ethnic pride. Oftentimes, there is overlap between rappers who are considered to be "positive" or "political," depending on the specific song. Positive rap can be considered to be prosocial and/or promoting messages that can contribute to the good of the individual listener or humanity. However, unlike political rap, positive rap may not have a political message or agenda. Positive rap tends to be value oriented. It may promote family values, diet (Dead Prez's Message to Eat Healthy), happiness (Dead Prez's Message to Be Happy), or other prosocial aspects. Positive rap is oftentimes referred to as the type of rap music parents do not mind their children listening to.

Another contemporary positive rap group is Black Eyed Peas, which have written songs about such topics as cause and effect in their song titled "Karma" on the *Behind the Front* CD:

> This is cause and effect
> The domino effect.

Black Eyed Peas also convey prosocial messages about maintaining love for humanity in their song "Where Is the Love" on their *Elephunk* CD, in which they question:

> What ever happen to the values of humanity.

There have been music labels that have attempted to gather a group of artists identified as more positive to form the identity of a record label. The late Rawkus Records is a good example of this. Currently, the Okay Players record label appears to be moving in this direction with artists such as The Roots, Common, Talib Kweli, and others.

As Nas states in "I Can," which is directed to young children, he informs the youth:

> If the truth is told the youth can grow.

Positive rap is the benchmark for rap therapy. The interesting thing about positive rap is that it is not necessarily a constant for specific rappers. Rather, positive rap manifests itself in a variety of different formats and on different songs, like Tupac's "Dear Mama," which is crowded by other not-so-positive songs on the CD. The best way to illustrate the educational and inspirational aspects of positive rap is to listen or read the lyrics of selected positive rap songs. The following is a list of some selected positive rap lyrics. A fuller listing is provided in appendix A.

The following is a list of some positive rap songs:

"War No More" by Wyclef Jean on *Masquerade* (2002).
"Daddy" by Wyclef Jean on *Masquerade* (2002).
"Memories Live" by Talib Kweli & Hitek on *Reflection Eternal* (2002).

"For Women" by Talib Kweli & Hitek on *Reflection Eternal*
    (2002).
"I Miss You" by DMX on *The Great Depression* (2001).
"A Minute for Your Sony" by DMX on *The Great Depression*
    (2001).

Rappers in this category often have eclectic jazz grooves play-ing with their music and may rap about seemingly abstract and irrelevant content. However, their music rarely crosses over to such a degree that it would be classified as gangsta rap. It may at times be political, but it is not necessarily defined as political rap as opposed to being positive or "conscious." The bridge of politi-cal and positive rap is also well illustrated by the music of the Native Tongues, who *Vibe* describes as good music about family, fun, and tolerance.

9. Spiritual Rap

Let us pray.
—DMX, "The Prayer" (*The Great Depression*)

Spiritual rap by artists such as Kirk Franklin incorporates rap music with traditional gospel music to appeal to many youth who would not otherwise listen to gospel music. Franklin's enlightened approach of incorporating rap into gospel to spread a religious message to urban youth influenced by rap music and the culture of hip-hop is in many ways similar to rap therapy's use of rap music to make traditional therapy and work with youth more accessible to those influenced by rap music. Franklin's merging of rap and gospel music has been successful and supported by many traditional rap artists such as Salt of Salt 'N' Pepa, who rapped on his hit single "Stomp" in 1997.

The spread of rap music to preachers' pulpits and gospel music is a good example of the infectiousness of rap music. However, many suggest that rap music, preaching, and/or orating all grow out of the same heritage. In fact, the Christian Church has become the home for several retired rappers who have become preachers. From the materialistic rap background as a P Diddy protégée, Mase retired from rap to become a preacher. Likewise, Run of Run DMC transitioned from the rap game to become a preacher in New York and M.C. Hammer became a reverend in

47

California. The similarity between rapping and preaching is un-
deniable. As mentioned earlier, many rappers are promoting messages that many in the Christian Church would consider to be
blasphemy; however, their method of sharing their words are similar. The relationship between rap music, preaching, and the church
in general is also seen by a large number of rappers who make
spiritual references in their rap songs, such as in "G.O.D. (Gaining
One's Definition)" by Common and "The Prayer" by DMX.
Recently, Connie Chung devoted a part of her show on CNN to
the murder of Jam Master J, the founder and DJ for Run DMC.
During a segment of one of CNN's reports, it was suggested that
Run DMC's lyrics were the closest thing to rap gospel, considering the many positive messages about which they rapped.

Although I mentioned in chapter 4 that there are six distinct
categories of rap music, it is unlikely that any one rapper fits exclusively in one category. A rapper's music often spans two or
more categories. Even gospel rappers can be heard making political statements, as is the case with many sermons. A good example
of a rapper whose music crosses several categories is the late
Tupac Shakur. Some of his music includes antisocial content common to gangsta rap. However, he also composed raps that can be
classified as materialistic, political, and positive. DMX is another
rapper whose raps span a broad cross section of classification. His
CD *Great Depression* includes songs that can be classified into all
five categories. As a result, DMX personifies the complexity, tex-
ture, and depth of rap music and many rap artists.

10. Rap Not Otherwise Specified

THE SIXTH category, which I call "Rap Not Otherwise Specified," is basically reserved for rap music that does not fit into one of the five categories described in chapter 4. This includes music that may simply add a rap hook or sample but is basically classified as rhythm and blues, rock, alternative, pop, jazz, or some other form of music. Artists that fit into this category are Usher and Jaheim, who are not considered rappers but are still a part of the hip-hop culture.

These different forms of rap music are the very reason why rap music has such a large appeal to a broad cross section of youth and adults. With this in mind, rap music has become the common ground for dialogue and conversation between youth and adults that may otherwise be separated by generation gaps that make communication and dialogue difficult.

Rap music's appeal to youth and young adults is very idiosyncratic. Many people like rap for the way its lyrical expression represents the reality of their lives and struggles. While some people are attracted to the messages promoted by rap music, others simply listen to the melodic beats initially and eventually take note of the lyrics or message. Regardless of the specific reasons for rap music's appeal, the important issue for those trying to communicate with youth or young adults, such as parents, teachers, and social service workers, is the realization of rap music's influence on a large cross section of society. Furthermore, rap music's appeal is not only consumed by youth. Rap music's appeal has grown to become intergenerational and cross-cultural.

Rap music is consumed through direct purchase, radio, Internet, graffiti images, posters, television, and video. Rap videos are available on a range of cable television stations throughout any given day. Rap artists have become household names for many people. Rap music's appeal to youth and young adults has been acknowledged and integrated into a variety of agendas.

Parents, teachers, and others interested in bridging the communication gap with those influenced by rap music would be wise to follow the lead of many major marketing companies. Marketers for clothing, beverages, and public service announcements about public health issues frequently utilize rap in their commercials to appeal to urban youth of color because they realize that rap is the language of those people who are members of the hip-hop culture. For example, as mentioned in chapter 9, gospel music producers such as Kirk Franklin have created a new genre of gospel music, which incorporates rap and hip-hop to appeal to youth and young adults. Developments such as this have culminated into what is now known as the culture of hip-hop. Rap music is simply the language of the culture of hip-hop, which is discussed in greater detail in the following chapter.

11. HIP-HOP CULTURE

As WITH any culture, those unfamiliar with hip-hop often feel a sense of culture shock when they are exposed to its different cultural norms. Culture is composed of symbols, language, values, and beliefs. Culture as defined by sociologists is a set of tangible and intangible elements that give shape and meaning to the everyday lives of a particular group of people. Culture is often broken down into two parts: material and nonmaterial. Material culture is composed of those tangible objects or things found within a culture. Within hip-hop culture, the dress or gear, language, behaviors, music, and symbols would be considered material culture. Some additional symbols of hip-hop include the art and style seen in such things as graffiti, jewelry, medallions, and poses. The language or communication of hip-hop is verbal and nonverbal. The language of hip-hop is rap music itself, which includes rhyme, rhythm, timing, syntax, and word structure.

The nonmaterial aspects of culture are composed of thoughts and beliefs. Nonmaterial aspects of hip-hop culture include beliefs such as those reflected in Public Enemy's lyrics "too black, too strong" and "fight the powers that be," KRS-1's lyrics "stop the violence" or "self-destruction, you're headed toward self-destruction,"

51

P Diddy's lyrics "it's all about the benjamins," and Queen Latifah's lyrics "U.N.I.T.Y." all symbolize some of the underlying beliefs of hip-hop culture. However, many of the values of hip-hop vary depending on such aspects as geography and orientation, as is seen in the different forms of rap music discussed in the previous chapters.

Culture provides the foundation for the development of community. Community is a group of people who are linked together by a variety of shared interests and identities. Hip-hop has several different communities, given the varying beliefs and orientations of its members and its multicultural membership. The different beliefs, values, and norms found within hip-hop culture are the aspects that give any culture its energy and dynamics.

Hip-hop as a culture is composed of individuals from diverse racial, ethnic, social, and economic backgrounds. Hip-hop's international appeal has expanded beyond the United States to the rest of the world. Hip-hop is "spoken" in many different languages. Its international appeal is seen through its production and consumption by Asian, European, African, and South American artists. The hip-hop community is defined through its artistic expression, which is manifested through its different yet similar forms of communication, dress, and musical identity.

When working with people from the hip-hop culture, one must speak their language. Just as one must know the native language of a foreign land when one travels abroad, one must also know the language of hip-hop to facilitate an effective dialogue with the many youth and young adults who are members of the hip-hop culture. As mentioned earlier, the language of the hip-hop culture is rap.

Unlike many cultures given by birthright, the culture of hip-hop is adopted. The reasons for adopting the culture are as diverse as are the people who migrate to hip-hop. One of the more common stories shared with me that explains this migration to the hip-hop culture includes becoming entranced by the melody and beat of the music. Others report that the lyrics speak to their experiences growing up in certain conditions, while some romanticize the lyrics of the rappers to which they enjoy listening, even though the lyrics do not express their experience.

Many people unfamiliar with hip-hop erroneously assume that it is composed of a group of inner-city misdirected youth. However, this misconception of hip-hop is far from the truth. The hip-hop culture is composed of people from diverse ethnic, gender, class, and educational backgrounds. Furthermore, recent reports on rap music sales indicate that the majority of people who purchase rap music are white, middle-class, suburban youth. During a recent report on CNN following the death of Jam Master Jay of Run DMC, a reporter suggested that the death of Jam Master Jay was comparable to the death of a member of the Beatles. If the Beatles can be considered the source of a cultural movement, then hip-hop would have to be considered a significant cultural format.

The culture of hip-hop also has its internal political struggles, as one genre disagrees with the beliefs of another. These differences of opinion began with debates between the East Coast rappers (e.g., Notorious B.I.G.) and the West Coast rappers (e.g., Tupac Shakur). The rap factions have grown to include a relatively new group of rappers known as the southern rappers, such as Master P, Jermain Dupri, Ludacris, and Outkast. These factions have heated debates and arguments just as intense as Democrats, Republicans, and Independents. A popular theme for many rappers concerns their editorial views about the state of the hip-hop culture, such as "I Used to Love Her" by Common Sense.

Rappers have also commonly used their music to convey a variety of political beliefs through their recordings, such as Louis

Farrakhan speaking in the transition between "Real Nigga Quotes" and "Retrospect for Life" on the CD *One Day It'll All Make Sense* by Common Sense. Furthermore, several hip-hop representatives have attempted to use their influence and understanding of the hip-hop culture to organize people. Russell Simmons, the CEO of Def Jam Records, has developed the Hip-Hop Summit. This is an annual meeting of members of the hip-hop community, including executives, producers, performers, educators, and politicians, to discuss and develop strategies for hip-hop to serve as a vehicle of political awareness and education.

The hip-hop culture has also become a popular theme for many motion pictures, such as *Brown Sugar* (2002), which describes the controversy of mainstream rap music, that enjoys increased sales versus underground rap music that may not be as popular but still attempts to promote positive messages, such as the late Rawkus record label. The film adaptation of the life story of rapper Eminem was depicted in *8 Mile* (2002). Other box-office movies depicting the culture of hip-hop include *Set It Off* (1996; which grossed over $36 million), *New Jack City* (1991; $47.6 million), *Bones* (2001; $7.3 million), and *Boyz N the Hood* (1991; $57.5 million). Other hit movies have starred rap artists such as Will Smith in *Independence Day* (1996), *Men in Black I* and *II* (1997, 2002), *Enemy of the State* (1998), *Wild Wild West* (1999), *Ali* (2001), and *Bad Boys I* and *II* (1995, 2003), and LL Cool J in *Any Given Sunday* (1999), *Deep Blue Sea* (1999), and *Halloween H2O* (1998). Many other rappers have made the transition to the big screen, such as DMX, Queen Latifah, Ice Cube, Snoop Doggy Dogg, Busta Rhymes, Method Man and Red Man, and Ja Rule, furthering the influence and notoriety of the hip-hop culture.

Parents, teachers, and those interested in learning more about the hip-hop culture and the rap music their children are listening to can utilize a variety of different approaches. Since the goal of rap therapy is to facilitate communication and dialogue between adults and children, the most ideal approach is to simply ask the person what songs he or she likes, why he or she likes them, and why he or she is listening to those particular songs. However, if this approach does not work, there are a variety of online resources that can inform you of the most popular songs and videos being played on national radio stations and video programs and selling at music stores. A short list of some resources available online are listed in appendix B.

The culture of hip-hop has not only grown from the large number of youth and young adults who enjoy listening to rap music, but is also in part due to the attention hip-hop has received from national political figures. As Michael Eric Dyson suggests, these two populations represent two extreme polarities in attitudes toward rap music. Several senators, educators, political activists, media commentators, and religious leaders promote attacks on the rap music industry. Considering some of the antisocial and sexist content of rap music, the political attacks and antagonism rap music receives is understandable. However, these attacks are in part responsible for the growing popularity, demand, and appreciation for rap music by many urban youth and young adults.

2 Live Crew, a rap group once based out of Florida, best illustrates this psychological reaction as a backlash to the political assault against rap music and the hip-hop culture. In 1989, the Florida governor began a political campaign attacking the content of 2 Live Crew's recordings. This political campaign led to a federal judge's decision to ban the sale of 2 Live Crew recordings to minors. Furthermore, many of the group's videos were banned as well. Following these political attacks, the group enjoyed one of their most lucrative years in total sales. The prohibition on the group's sales to youth created a state of psychological reactance

and motivated youth to find means of obtaining copies of their recordings. The governor had in effect created a greater demand for the music he was attempting to stifle. This is an important point for many parents, educators, and others who would like the children or young adults they work with to stop listening to rap music. If the prohibition becomes too strong, the opposite effect may be produced. It is probably a better idea to utilize a person's interest in rap music to facilitate greater communication, dialogue, and insight. This is the goal of rap therapy.

PART 2

THEORY

12. THE FORERUNNERS TO RAP THERAPY

THE USE of culturally or developmentally appropriate mediums of communication with clients is a very common technique used by therapists. Play therapy is a good example of using "play" in therapy with children to build a therapeutic relationship. As early as 1928, Anna Freud and Melanie Klein wrote extensively about their use of play with children to help them work through issues of trauma. Many psychologists such as Charles Schaefer continue to research and apply play in the treatment of their young clients. Rap therapy's use of rap music to help clients work through emotional or behavioral difficulties is similar.

Music therapy, art therapy, and expressive therapy have acknowledged the significant influence of music and art on people's perceptions, beliefs, behaviors, and emotions for many years. Music plays an important role in our society. Tribute to American Heroes, a musical fund-raiser to support relief efforts following the September 11, 2001, terrorist acts on America, reportedly raised over $100 million. Conversely, during the weeks and months following the attacks, several radio stations banned the playing of certain songs because they "compromise the national healing process." The value of music is acknowledged and used in a broad range of activities and places, including inaugurations, opening sports events, religious ceremonies, weddings, doctors' offices, and elevators.

Through recognizing the significant influence of music on humanity, music therapists have utilized music therapeutically to help address cognitive, emotional, and behavioral functioning for many years. Music therapy is also used to help with issues related to treatment of cancer, substance abuse, and chronic pain. People who listen to music for its soothing qualities, to relax, or induce certain emotional states are using music therapeutically.

Expressive writing through poetry, rap, or a journal is found to cause improvements in health and psychological well-being. This is done by improving one's ability to cope with stress. James Pennhaher, a psychologist at the University of Texas, finds results on the curative effects of this type of creative writing.

In addition to utilizing different tools such as toys, music, and writing to help clients resolve different presenting issues, psychologists have also recently begun focusing on the importance of integrating cultural sensitivity into their work with clients. Given the significance that culture plays on one's outlook, perceptions, beliefs, behaviors, and norms, culturally sensitive treatment is now an integral part of the work in which many psychologists are involved.

Culturally Sensitive Therapy

Many psychologists once thought that all people were basically the same and that whatever results were obtained from research with one set of individuals could easily be generalizable to people everywhere. Since most psychologists conducting research in the United States and Europe tend to work in university settings, most research utilizes university and college students as samples. However, most university and college settings are not a microcosm of the larger society because of the limited diversity found in these settings.

The tendency for psychologists to use university and college students as samples has raised important questions and concerns for some contemporary psychologists promoting the value of cultural sensitivity in psychological research and clinical practice. They argue that results obtained from research done with a homogenous group of college and university students cannot always be generalized to people from other cultures such as Latin Americans or African Americans who do not attend college. Sociocultural factors affect what people learn through experience. Sociocultural variables include such factors as social identity, gender, ethnicity, race, religion, sexual orientation, and social class. Each of these variables creates significant differences in behaviors and mental processes, especially across different cultures. These concerns have given rise to a movement to promote culturally sensitive research and clinical practice in the field of psychology.

The concept of cultural sensitivity in psychotherapy and counseling has recently received a lot of attention in clinical settings as well as in educational settings. In the area of mental health, "cultural sensitivity," "cultural competence," "cultural relevance," "multiculturalism," and "diversity" have become the catch phrases heard throughout the country. This is due in part to multiple demographic changes currently taking place in American society that are contributing to significant increases in the cultural diversity of the country. With respect to the growing cultural diversity currently taking place in American demography, there has been a significant growth rate of Asian American, Latino, and other ethnic minority groups in America since 1986. According to the U.S. Department of Labor and Commerce, these rates of increase are expected to continue within the foreseeable future.

Diversity as a concept is complex due to both the breadth and depth of the heterogeneity it encompasses. Diversity has historically been considered through the variables of race, ethnicity, culture, gender, sexual orientation, age, education, religious orientation, and ability. However, all these differences can be considered dimensions of diversity. Considering the multiple barriers in direct and indirect communication created by the growing cultural diversity in America, mental health workers have begun to realize the need to develop cultural competence if they are to maintain the efficacy of their treatment.

The need for counseling to be sensitive to one's culture is very important. When speaking with youth, it is important to acknowledge the influence and value that culture has on their life and views. This is not only true for people of color, but also applies to cultural differences between whites, who may be seen as being similar even though they have different cultural backgrounds. Everyone has a cultural background that shapes his or her outlook on life. Just as an Italian American may have different cultural values from a Puerto Rican, people influenced by hip-hop culture may have different cultural norms than those influenced by the hippie culture of Woodstock. The value of considering one's culture when attempting to improve communication is illustrated by the opening quote in the introduction to this book by an African American twenty-year-old client speaking of culturally insensitive therapists, "They don't understand that what they are saying is going in one ear and out the other, it just gives me a headache when I go in there, I just want to get out and go get high, because it does not help me at all."

Rap therapy attempts to validate the experiences, beliefs, and values of youth influenced by rap music and hip-hop as a culturally sensitive approach to treatment.

Psychologists have a long history of developing different approaches to improve the effectiveness of their work with clients. As most people who work with children and young adults know, it can be very difficult to form a good working relationship with them. After years of being frustrated by the inadequacy of conventional methods of engagement with clients, I decided it was necessary to develop new strategies.

I began thinking of different strategies to improve my work with people influenced by the culture of hip-hop. I noticed that many of the clients who came to my office arrived reciting the lyrics of their favorite rap song. After discussing the songs with them, it became clear to me that the songs were in many ways metaphorically significant and related to the clinical issues that brought them into treatment. With this in mind, I began to critically analyze the relationship of the rap songs clients would come in reciting in relation to their psychological issues. Hence, the concept of rap therapy was developed.

Given that the influence of rap and hip-hop on most people is through learning and positive reinforcement, the theoretical model of rap therapy was influenced by the works of social learning theorists such as Neal Miller and John Dollard, who suggest that imitation is taught through basic learning principles of stimulus, reward, and response. Furthermore, Albert Bandura's broader reformulation of social learning theory suggests that learning and imitation also occur through the observation of models. Another social psychology theory that can be utilized to understand the impact that rap music has had on the socialization of urban youth of color is field theory. This theory suggests that behavior is a function of both the person and the environment.

Rap music as a stimulus is modeled in the environment of many youth and young adults directly by peers and media images and reinforced in the narratives of materialistic lyrics. Rap therapy neither endorses nor admonishes rap music's presence and influence on youth and young adults. Rap therapy is utilized as a tool by culturally sensitive therapists who acknowledge the influence that rap music has on youth and young adults. For the rap therapist, rap music is a tool that can be utilized in the service of counseling and educating youth and young adults.

13. RAP THERAPY

THERAPISTS, PARENTS, teachers, and counselors who work with youth and young adults who are influenced by rap music can use rap therapy as a means of promoting positive behavioral change and improved insight into their lives. Rap therapy is best conducted by following a certain approach. The approach includes the following five steps:

1. Assess the person's interest in rap music and hip-hop (clothing, videos, concerts, and so on) and develop a plan for using rap music with the person.
2. Build a relationship and alliance with the person through discussing the different types of rap songs to which he or she enjoys listening.
3. Challenge the person with the lyrics of his or her rap icons to reevaluate his or her thoughts and behaviors.
4. Ask the person to write raps about the desired change you have set up as a goal for him or her.
5. Monitor and maintain the progress made through continued discussions and feedback.

These steps are adapted from the rap therapy model that includes the following five phases:

1. Assess and plan
2. Build alliance
3. Reframe thoughts and behavior
4. Reinforce through writing
5. Maintain the change

The phases of rap therapy may proceed in order or they may fluctuate as well.

Assess and Plan

To best illustrate the point of assessing and planning, consider the case of Mike. Mike is a twenty-year-old young man I worked with using rap therapy to help him improve his anger management skills. When Mike first visited my office, I conducted my customary intake by getting some background information and an extensive history of the problem that brought him to my office, such as his work/educational background, medical history, family history, legal history, and information on any medication/drugs he was currently taking or had taken in the past. After finishing this rather structured interview, I asked him about his hobbies and pastimes. Mike informed me that he enjoyed listening to rap music and playing basketball and video games. I followed up with his interest in rap music and asked the following questions:

Which rap artists do you enjoy listening to?
Why do you enjoy listening to these particular rap artists?
What is your favorite rap song?

Why is this your favorite rap song?

What is your favorite rap/hip-hop video?

Why is this your favorite rap/hip-hop video?

Which rap artist don't you like?

Why don't you like this particular rap artist?

In rap therapy, questions such as these form the foundation for assessing the person's interests and influence by rap and hip-hop. The goal of the assessment stage is to determine if the person that you plan to work with is significantly influenced by rap music.

For me, the assessment stage serves two purposes. First, it allows me to move away from the scripted interview I conduct to get some background information to discuss topics about which the client feels much more comfortable speaking. By asking questions about a person's hobbies, you allow him or her to put his or her guard down and form a relationship with you from an area of familiarity and comfort. Second, the assessment allows me to determine how much rap music influences the client's life and if it has any relationship to why he or she has come to visit me. In the case of Mike, it was significant to find out that he only listened to gangsta rap, which reinforced his difficulty with managing his anger.

As I began to plan how we could use rap music as a tool for improving his anger management skills, I knew I had to help him transition from listening only to gangsta rap. He would have to begin listening to other forms of rap that did not reinforce his problems with anger. Furthermore, I knew I had to find a gangsta rap artist Mike enjoyed listening to who spoke about the importance of managing anger.

This example about Mike's case outlines the strategy and process of assessing the influence of rap and hip-hop on someone's life and provides some of the thoughts behind the development of a plan to use rap music to promote behavior change.

Building Alliance

I am afraid to tell you who I am, because, if I tell you who I am, you may not like who I am, and it's all that I have.

—John Powell

Developing and maintaining alliance is about relationship building and it is one of the most critical steps in any productive working relationship. During the alliance stage, the primary goal is to develop a strong working relationship with the person by being empathic and supportive of his or her interest in rap music. During this phase, it is important to invite the client to introduce you to his or her favorite rap songs and listen to the songs with him or her. When I asked Mike to bring his favorite rap songs to our following meeting, he was both shocked and encouraged— shocked by my interest and encouraged that I was willing to be entertained in the same way he entertained himself. He later reported that my asking him to bring his favorite rap CDs to our next appointment made him feel "heard" and affirmed. These are two very important variables in relationship building.

Mike came to the next appointment ten minutes early with two different Tupac Shakur CDs. We began the session by listening to "Hit 'Em Up." The song contains some very angry and antisocial lyrics. After listening to the song, we discussed the lyrics in the song and why Mike selected this song to listen to with me and what it was about this song that he enjoyed. Mike informed me that he enjoyed this song because it was similar to the situations with which he found himself regularly confronted in his community and he thought it would be informative for me to hear the lyrics. What he did not tell me was that the song was as much about him assessing me as it was of me assessing him. My reaction to the song and him would inform him how open and trustworthy I would be with hearing his own stories. He later told me that after we listened to the song together and saw that it did not "shake me," he knew he "could keep it real" in his discussions with me. Mike's point is very important because by listening to the rap music together, he was able to determine my response to provocative content without revealing much about himself before he began sharing personal information with me.

The value of listening to rap songs with clients and discussing the content with them in an open nonjudgmental way is incredibly affirming for someone from this culture. It is important to be open, nonjudgmental, and affirming in your discussions of rap with them. By being open and nonjudgmental, you allow them to speak to you without getting offended or defensive about the topics they present. By affirming their interests, you allow them to become open and truthful in their discussions with you. The song they present on the first session is usually just the tip of the iceberg, but it begins the development of a mutual understanding and supportive relationship that is built on trust. This is the foundation of building a good working relationship with the client and it is necessary for the latter stages of rap therapy. As with the assessment stage, maintaining a good working relationship is an ongoing part of your work together.

Reframe Thoughts and Behavior

The goal of this stage is to challenge the client to broaden his or her appreciation of rap to include other forms that do not reinforce his or her problem behavior or thoughts. In the case of Mike, I began by discussing songs by Tupac that where not angry, antisocial, and violent. We discussed Tupac's "Dear Mama," "Unconditional Love," and "Keep Your Head Up," all of which speak about the value of mother-child relationships and the importance of African American men valuing the relationships of both their mothers in particular and women in general. After discussing the content of these songs with Mike, he was able to begin speaking about other songs he enjoyed that did not reinforce his anger. I reinforced his appreciation for these nonangry songs and discussed the relationship they had to his situation.

Rap music is very diverse in its content. It ranges from antisocial, sexist, racist, and misogynistic messages, to prosocial, uplifting, self-empowering, and spiritual messages. As in the case of Mike, the person may first report that he or she only enjoys listening to angry gangsta rap. However, one must have a certain level of comfort with this antisocial content in order to eventually alter the person's rap interest to include positive or educational lyrics in rap music. A comfort level with the antisocial content of rap music can be developed by keeping in mind what the ultimate goal of using rap music in conversations and educational exercises with youth is. The goal is to use rap music to teach youth lessons that may otherwise be difficult to teach because of the content or because they are not willing to listen to the lesson since they think it does not apply to them or it is too out of date.

For instance, it may be difficult to speak about the dangers of guns to teenagers who live in gang-infested neighborhoods and who value the lifestyle of gang bangers. However, by listening to a rap song by an artist that they enjoy listening to, you may be able to use one of their songs to help them gain some insight into the dangers of guns. If they like an artist like 50 Cents, a conversation about the number of times he has been shot could change their opinions about the dangers of hanging out with gang bangers. Likewise, one of his songs that speaks about the dangers of being shot could be used to teach a similar lesson.

Another way to gain an appreciation and tolerance for using

rap music to improve conversations and education with youth is to think of the value of having them listen to rap music that does not promote antisocial messages. However, to get to this transition, one may have to initially listen to the antisocial music with them and then incorporate some prosocial rap music into the conversation. With this in mind, another goal of rap therapy is to generalize a person's appreciation of rap music so that it is not exclusively the antisocial or sexist type of rap, but also includes the prosocial and positive forms of rap. This is exemplified in the work I did with Mike by discussing some prosocial songs by Tupac.

As in the case of Tupac, there can be great variability in the content of the lyrics of a rap artist from song to song. The diversity found in the lyrics of an artist from song to song speaks to the multiple interests of the artist. Since we all have multiple interests, these contradictory messages can be used therapeutically to help people integrate and understand their own conflicting interests and desires.

This is best understood by considering my work with many urban youth who do not value education and school. Oftentimes, students argue from the perspective that education is worthless or inconsistent with their ideas of being street smart, hip, cool, or "chillin'." However, after challenging this concept with prosocial lyrics by artists who they enjoy listening to and identify as primarily having gangsta lyrics, it is possible to change students' thoughts in a way that is not possible with the lyrics of rappers who are known to rap about prosocial concepts exclusively. Thus, in many ways gangsta rap artists may have more credibility for challenging and restructuring many youths' ideas and behaviors.

After successfully reframing clients' thoughts and behaviors by challenging them with the lyrics of different rap artists, I attempt to have them write their own raps or poems. This begins the transition into the fourth phase of rap therapy.

Reinforce Through Writing

The primary goal of this stage is to get clients more actively involved in their treatment by having them begin to write their own raps or poems about the desired change in their behavior or thoughts. In Mike's case, I began by asking him if he had ever written any raps. He had, so I asked him if he would share one of his raps with me at our next meeting. He agreed and the following week he returned to my office with a rap he had written. An excerpt from his rap read:

> Big niggas like you I don't fight
> Niggas like you run in fright
> 'Cause they get shot
> Don't call my bluff
> Or I'll guarantee that bullet to the dome
> Did you forget, I know where you be at
> I know where you rest at
> And the location of your kids' schools
> Snatch 'em up and then size 'em for cement shoes
> Yeah, I ain't gonna let it rest
> Until I let six off in your chest plate.

I thanked Mike for being courageous enough to share the rap with me and applauded his creativity. He immediately began to explain the context of the rap and how he really did not have any intentions on hurting the person about which the rap was written. We continued to talk about the rap and the situation and I provided him with some feedback on how to manage his anger and the situation without violence. As we concluded the session, I asked him if he thought he could write a rap about managing his anger without violence and he said he would try. The following week he returned with a rap that read:

Ain't it a shame when our lil' kid's banging
on the corner slanging
I did the same when I was out there
Until change came in
We all have the same skin
And I gotta stop blamin
Deal with the pain
And the shame of being insane
Become a man that can remain tame.

I applauded his effort and creativity; he laughed and began discussing the rap. I reinforced the dramatic shift in his thoughts about anger and continued to refer back to this rap in our work together.

Once you are able to get the person to write a rap that is a shift from his or her baseline thought process, it becomes the anchor for the rest of your work together. The shift in Mike's thinking was very powerful because it became his vision and determination for change. He had finally taken on the responsibility of wanting to improve his anger management skills as opposed to having it be the interest of some external source.

During the following weeks, Mike continued to write raps about managing his anger and he shared them with me. For several weeks, our work together included him doing homework that included writing raps about different topics and our subsequent discussions of those raps in the following meetings. The raps Mike wrote about were in response to my asking him if he could write a rap about:

Why it is important to control your anger?

Why do people with problems with anger get into trouble?

How can people control their anger?

How can people express their anger functionally?

How do you plan to control your anger?

As in the first rap that Mike wrote on managing his anger, each subsequent rap was just as insightful and powerful. I continued to reinforce and praise his efforts. Mike reported that his anger management was progressively improving and his parents were able to confirm his reports. After a client begins to make substantial changes in his or her behavior, the goal of your work together transitions into maintaining the progress.

Maintain the Change

Maintaining the person's therapeutic change is facilitated through ongoing reinforcement. An assessment of the actual success of altering a person's thoughts or behavior can be determined by asking the person directly in an interview or through a self-report questionnaire. I often use such questionnaires as pre- and postassessments in my work with different clients. For example, a questionnaire to assess a person's anger would include the following:

1. How long have you been dealing with difficulties in managing your anger?
2. How often do you get angry every week?
3. What do you do when you get angry?
4. Have you hurt anyone while angry?
5. How many fights do you get into every week?
6. Has your anger led to involvement with the police?

These questions can be used as a pre- and postscreen to determine if a person has gained any better control over managing his or her anger. The goal is to decrease the frequency of angry outbursts as well as the detrimental consequences of having limited control over angry impulses.

The assessment may also involve gaining collateral information from teachers, parents, or other people who may monitor the person's improvement. The model of rap therapy is easy to follow and apply. It can easily be used by people who are not therapists, such as parents and teachers, to facilitate change in behavior and thoughts of those who are part of the hip-hop culture. Change should also be maintained by the insight gained through the other stages of the model. As one becomes more insightful to the unconscious effects and influences that antisocial lyrics may have on his or her behavior or outlook on life, he or she usually becomes less impressionable. The insight gained allows one to defend against the negative messages in many rap songs. Hence, once a client's thoughts and behaviors are reframed, he or she is oftentimes able to reinforce and maintain his or her own positive development. As I finished working with one young woman who fondly referred to herself as a "hip-hop junkie," she said:

> I can't believe I used to listen to the lyrics in some of these songs and not pay any attention to them. I used to sing along with the song calling myself a bitch and hoe, like it was a good thing or some type of badge of honor. I am happy that those types of lyrics don't just slip under the radar like they used to. Especially since I have a daughter of my own, how would I sound being a mother singing about bitches and hoes with my daughter sitting on my lap.

PART 3

RAP THERAPY IN ACTION

In the following chapters, ten case studies of the successful use of rap therapy are presented. The case studies range in presenting issues from anger management, to dealing with loss and grief. In each of the cases, rap music or aspects of hip-hop culture was the driving force behind the cognitive and behavioral change that took place for each individual. Several significant demographic aspects have been altered to maintain confidentiality. The goal of presenting these case studies is to provide the reader with a better understanding of the use of rap music to create positive change and the process in which this change may occur.

14. JOHN AND ANGER MANAGEMENT

Expressing My Anger Through Words
A Case of Anger Management Through Rap

JOHN, a seventeen-year-old African American, made an appointment to visit my office following the recommendation of his guidance counselor after several angry outbursts in high school with teachers and staff. Escorted by his mother, John arrived on time and well dressed for his first appointment. He was articulate, insightful, and easy to speak with. He was in his senior year of high school at a local public school. He had never had any major medical or drug problems and had never been seen by a therapist. His mother raised John as the only child in a single-parent middle-class family. He reported that he had always had a supportive relationship with his mother, but his relationship with his father had always been strained. Through his sophomore year in high school, John was a good student with a B+ grade point average. His mother reported that during his junior year his grades began to drop, he started hanging out with "the wrong" group of kids, and he began having behavior problems in school. In general, John was a relatively well-adjusted teenager with the exception of the reported anger management difficulties.

Chief Complaint

After asking what precipitated the visit John replied, "I guess it's because I have been getting into a lot of altercations at school with my teachers." His mother added, "He has become so angry over the past year and won't tell us why." When asked if he was angry, John simply shrugged his shoulders and looked out the window as if he was daydreaming. After further questioning, John was able to admit that he was having difficulties managing his anger. He was not sure of the cause of his recent angry outbursts, but he wanted some help in developing skills to manage his anger better.

During our next visit, John arrived casually dressed and on time. I asked if he would mind completing an anger management survey so that I could better understand the severity and frequency of his anger management difficulties. He readily agreed to complete the ten-question survey. He reported that he had been angry more than ten times in the past week and that his anger had manifested in physical symptoms, such as headaches, stomach pains, and fatigue. He also confirmed that he had gotten into multiple arguments in the past week due to his anger.

Hobbies

I asked John to tell me a bit about his hobbies and what he enjoyed doing in his spare time. He reported that he loved to play video games on his Playstation 2 and Xbox. Not surprisingly, his favorite games were fighting games. He did not have any insight into why his favorite games were those with violent and confrontational themes. He also reported that he loved listening to rap music and had over 500 rap CDs at home. He did not appear to have a favorite rap artist or like a specific type of rap music. He enjoyed listening to both male and female artists. He listened to gangsta rap as well as prosocial rap. He often referred to himself as a student of the "rap game." I told him that I was involved in researching the use of rap music in therapy and would like to discuss different rap themes and music with him in our work together. He was particularly happy to find out about this interest and responded, "That's tight, we will be able to speak the same language then."

Course of Treatment

Over the course of eleven weeks together, John and I incorporated rap music into our discussions and work together. He was particularly knowledgeable about the history and sociology of the rap music culture and educated me on a great deal of factors of which I was not aware. Since John was so interested in rap, I asked him if he would be willing to write a rap about his feelings of anger so that I could understand his experience a bit better. He happily agreed and left my office smiling.

The following week John arrived and said I got some "shit for you Doc." I said, "I'm all ears, let me hear some of your skills." He read the following excerpt from a rap he wrote during the previous week.

> *Anger changes atmospheres, attitudes and the look on my face,*
> *blood pulsating,*
> *fist all balled ready to blast a blow*
> *mouth spitting fire, it's hot straight smoking*
> *arms flapping*
> *I ain't joking*
> *Damn sure ain't coping.*

After reading the rap, he immediately began explaining the content of what he wrote. He reported that his first reaction when he gets angry is physical. I immediately utilized this insight as an anchor for helping John notice his own warning signs. I began questioning him in such a way that he would begin to gain further insight into these signs. The following dialogue took place:

> Dr. E: Do you think you notice your blood pulsating, your fist clenching, and the look on your face changing as you are becoming angry?
>
> John: Absolutely.
>
> Dr. E: Do you think the physical changes you experience could help you notice that you are becoming angry?
>
> John: Yeah, that's what I'm saying Dr. E.
>
> Dr. E. What do you think you could do in response to your body telling you you're getting angry?
>
> John: I guess I could take a walk and try to cool down.
>
> Dr. E: That sounds like a good coping strategy, do you have any other ideas?
>
> John: I don't know.
>
> Dr. E: Okay, that's fine, I will review some other relaxation techniques you can use when you find yourself getting angry. In your rap, you mentioned you did not think you were coping well, let's talk about what you can do to feel more confident in your coping ability.
>
> John: Sounds good to me.

Our conversation on developing different coping skills continued. The important piece in this part of the discussion on John is that by utilizing rap music as a catalyst we were able to begin speaking about his problem with anger management. After reviewing some coping strategies with John, we ended our session together by talking about some of the factors that contribute to him getting angry. I asked him if he would write a rap for our next session that spoke to the cause or triggers of his anger.

The following week he arrived at my office excited and eager once again to read what he had written. He read the following excerpt from his rap on the causes of his anger:

> *My eyes are open but I can't see*
> *when, where, why anger is coming at me,*
> *meet a girl as she walks my way,*
> *she throws her nose up and walks away*
> *I'm angry*
> *A brother calls his goddess a bitch*
> *five minutes ago it was all love, hugs, and a kiss*
> *I'm angry.*

Through following up on the second rap, John and I were able to discuss how insightful he was to understand at such a young age the volatility of his emotional world. From his words—"my eyes are open but I can't see / when, where, why anger is coming at me"—I was able to open a discussion with him about the dynamic nature of the emotional world. He was pleased to find out that it is "normal" to have multiple emotional experiences through the course of a day. By being understanding and normalizing his experience, he became further willing to discuss other aspects of his anger and emotional life.

I was also able to help John realize that although there may be many paradoxes in life that are upsetting or irritating, such as those he mentions in his rap, it is also important to recognize the irrelevance many of these things have on his life. By not personalizing each minor frustration he experiences, he will be better prepared to avoid the intense anger it may cause him. This led to a discussion about the minor differences between emotions on the continuum of anger. For John, there was simply life without anger and then anger. We discussed the differences between anger and frustration, irritation, disappointment, and daily hassles.

I asked if there were situations closer or more personal to him that caused anger. In our discussions, it became evident that John harbored significant animosity and resentment toward his father, which fueled much of his anger. For our next session together, I asked if he could write a rap about his "disappointment" in his relationship with his father. The following week he arrived with the following truncated version of his rap:

> *It's me your lil' seed dun,*
> *Your lil' son*
> *I'll put the bullshit aside,*
> *I'm trying to see ya*
> *Let me know when, and where*
> *I don't need no hoes, no clothes,*
> *no shit that glistens*
> *If you know everything,*
> *Then where is that shit I've been missin'.*

After reading the third rap, John said, "Now I feel angry, I ain't frustrated, disappointed, or irritated. I'm just angry." Apparently, after five weeks of discussing his anger management issues, John had finally gotten to one of the primary causes of his anger. The following discussion transpired:

Dr. E.: Why do you think you are so angry now?

John: 'Cause, man, that rap made me angry. It made me angry when I was writing it.

Dr. E.: Help me understand why writing the rap made you angry.

John: 'Cause, it reminded me about my father, and you know, he is never there for me. When I call him he does not call me back, when we are suppose to get together and do something he fakes and I'm just at home waiting. When I do see him, he always wants to tell me what I should be doing and he ain't even doing what he should be doing. C'mon man, I'm his son, he don't even return my calls.

Dr. E.: I understand why that would make you angry.

John: Yeah I'm angry, my own pop's don't want to fuck with me.

Dr. E.: What do you think that means?

John: I told you the first time I wrote one of these raps, females don't want to be bothered by me, I can't blame them, my own father don't want to be bothered with me either.

The conversation continued and we were able to further discuss the implications of his failed relationship with his father. We also discussed how he generalized this experience to many of his interpersonal relationships, which ultimately compromised the development of productive and genuine relationships. We spent the next four weeks talking about his relationship with his father and how to put it into proper perspective so that it did not color all of his relationships. By giving John a creative output and an opportunity to gain further insight into his arrested interpersonal development, he was able to gain better control over his anger. Rap music provided the medium for this discussion to take place. John's anger progressively decreased after he was able to gain greater insight into the cause and maintain the source of his anger.

At the conclusion of our tenth visit together, I asked John if he could write a rap about the benefits or insight he had gained during our work together. The following week he read the following original rap:

> *In managing anger, I got an idea what to do*
> *I ain't got it perfected, but I gotta clue*
> *It's not real simple like one plus two*
> *But I know how to body slam anger when it tries to pursue*
> *I find someone to talk to*
> *From B, and D to T*
> *The list goes on and on*
> *And even if everyone's gone.*
> *God's with me.*

During our work together, John and I discussed how managing anger and other emotions required the development of a broad range of coping strategies. We discussed how one strategy such as deep breathing may work in one scenario, while taking a walk may work best in another, and so on. John began to understand that managing anger is a complex task that did not have one simple solution that would always work for every situation. When he wrote "[i]n managing anger, I got an idea what to do / I ain't got it perfected, but I gotta clue," he made it clear that he had gained significant insight into the complexities of managing anger.

John and I continued to work together for two more weeks. At the conclusion of our therapeutic relationship, his angry outbursts had disappeared for four weeks. He continued to experience anger and frustration, but he had begun to reach a point in his emotional development where he was able to manage his anger in a functional and appropriate manner. John's frustration and difficulty in his relationship with his father did not get resolved during our work together.

Postscript

John decided he did not want to reach out and call his father. However, by uncovering the source of his anger and frustration, he was able to give his pain a voice, which allowed him to begin the healing process. His angry outbursts slowly abated until they were extinguished for four weeks straight. He wrote that the benefits he received through using rap music to help provide insight and resolution to his conflict were many.

One of the most striking aspects of John's recovery was revealed in his posttreatment assessment survey. He reported that on average his anger had decreased from more than ten episodes a week to less than four episodes a week. John no longer had any physical symptoms that accompanied his anger or were caused by his anger. Furthermore, he reported that the use of rap music helped him develop a level of insight that he did not believe would have been accomplished without the use of listening, discussing, and writing about different themes through the medium of rap.

15. YOLANDA

Rapping Against Depression
A Case on Self-Hatred

YOLANDA WAS an eighteen-year-old woman who phoned for an appointment at a metropolitan community health center. For her first appointment, she wore baggy jeans, a white Pelle Pelle sweater, and a pair of black Lugz with thick soles. Her hair was braided and she walked with a slight drag in her step, as if she were mimicking a pimp in a 1970s blaxploitation film. She was forty pounds overweight and spoke in a deep voice. She began her conversation by informing me that she "really is not into this therapy stuff," but she had to talk to somebody.

Yolanda was the product of a broken family. She had never met her father and reported that her mother died when she was three years old. She was unclear about the cause of her mother's death, but other family members suggested that it was due to a stroke. Following the death of her mother, Yolanda was raised by her grandmother in a "drug-infested" urban housing project. She had one older brother and a younger sister, with whom she said she had a strained relationship.

Chief Complaint

"I gotta talk to somebody, 'cause I'm living in darkness" is how she opened the conversation. After further questioning, Yolanda revealed that she had problems falling asleep, increased appetite (which led to twenty pounds of weight gain in six months), avoided friends, and spent most hours of the day indoors behind closed blinds. Two months after graduating from high school, she moved out of her grandmother's house because of eight months of regular arguing about smoking marijuana in her bedroom. She was currently living with a friend and wanted to find a job but had not begun the search process.

History of Chief Complaint

Yolanda reported that she had always felt depressed. She reported that as a little girl she was always unhappy and could not understand why her friends had a mother and a father and she did not. She said she did not think she was worthy of "parents." Her relationship with her grandmother was "okay, but it's not the type of relationship you have with your own mother or father."

Yolanda began smoking marijuana when she was fourteen years old. She was unable to articulate why she began smoking other than to say, "C'mon now, you gotta ask why I smoke weed, then maybe I need to talk to somebody else." Yolanda said that she had never had any suicidal thoughts and was against taking any medication. She did not have any medical problems, had never been arrested, and was an average student in school.

Hobbies

Yolanda's hobbies included "parties, dancing, and watching music videos." Her favorite type of music was rap. She indicated that her favorite rap CD was *Great Depression* by DMX. When asked why she liked *Great Depression*, she immediately responded by saying, "He [DMX] knows about struggle, loss of family members, and like the name of the CD, he can relate to depression. Plus the beats are bangin' and I like the poetry pieces he does without any beats. The brother is real."

Given the symbolic relationship of Yolanda's diagnostic presentation of a major depressive disorder and the title of her favorite rap CD, I was able to bridge a discussion and a relationship around her hobby.

Course of Treatment

Given that rap music and hip-hop were two of the few hobbies that persisted as interests for Yolanda during her depressive episodes, we began our relationship by talking about her interest in rap music. During our next couple of meetings together, we had our customary discussion about her symptoms of depression and the severity of her social withdrawal. I reviewed different coping strategies she could try using as we worked on developing a treatment plan to resolve her depressive episodes. I encouraged her to avoid drug use and engage in drug-free hobbies. I also discussed other coping strategies that she might consider, such as taking walks during the day, opening the blinds in her house to be exposed to greater amounts of sunlight, getting more exercise, improving her diet, and spending time with friends. However, most of our hourly once-a-week discussions centered around rap music.

I learned as many details as possible about her interest in rap music. I encouraged her to bring music to her sessions with me. We would listen to selected songs and discuss the content of the music. She would explain why she liked a particular song and I would listen and discuss this interest with her in an open and nonjudgmental way. As discussed earlier, by developing a level of comfort with using rap music as a catalyst for conversation and educational discussions about different topics, one is able to use rap music in a way that is nonjudgmental. By using rap and the culture of hip-hop in a nonjudgmental way with clients who are influenced by the hip-hop culture, you are able to gain their trust and influence them.

At the conclusion of our fourth session together, I informed Yolanda that I thought it would be beneficial if she began keeping a journal. She agreed. For her first entry in her journal, I asked her to write a rap on self-love. Despite her depressive symptoms, I was surprised to see that she openly agreed to the request without any coaxing or need for clarification.

The following week she arrived at my office with her journal in hand and ready to read what she had written. She seemed to be very excited. Our session began with her reading the following rap:

Self-love is the loving feeling I get when I am with my child
Self-love is something I don't think many people understand
Love is sweet,
Love is kind,
Love is gentle,
Love is me loving me
  More than I love you
Love is a feeling within the soul.

By using the language of "rap" to speak with Yolanda, I had opened a door of communication that allowed her to be authentic in a way that traditional dialogue left closed. Through her rap, she revealed and opened a curative door for treatment to proceed through. The rest of the session was spent providing positive reinforcement for her rap and discussing the meaning behind it. I was able to provide positive reinforcement by applauding her efforts, her level of insight that she gained, and her willingness to share each of her writings. By simply encouraging her and telling her what a good job she was doing and how insightful she was becoming, she was able to develop a level of self-efficacy in managing her emotions that she had not had in the past.

I was able to challenge her to begin thinking about why her self-love was dependent on the presence of her daughter. We discussed why she believed that self-love is something not many people understand. Through this discussion, Yolanda was able to realize that self-love was something she did not understand and that she was projecting this belief onto others as a way of rationalizing her fear of self-love. I was able to challenge her to consider loving herself for who she was as an individual independent of her daughter. This rap proved to be the anchor and turning point for the rest of our work together.

After discussing her rap on self-love, I asked Yolanda to complete a self-esteem assessment (see Figure 1 on page 94). The self-esteem assessment simply allows a person to rate from 1 (low) to 10 (high) how they currently perceive their self-esteem and what they hope their self-esteem will be in the future. Yolanda rated her current self-esteem as a 4 and her goal was a 9 at the conclusion of treatment. We concluded the session with Yolanda agreeing to write a rap for our next session about how she planned to improve her self-esteem.

Figure 1. Self-Esteem Rating

	CURRENT	GOAL
10		
9		X
8		
7		
6		
5		
4	X	
3		
2		
1		

The following week Yolanda arrived at my office ten minutes early and eager to read her new rap. The following is a truncated version of what she wrote:

All of my life I have done nothing but put other things in front of me,
Drugs, violence, having a daughter, and friends or so-called friends,
I ended up in so many dark holes. . . .
I wore baggy clothes to hide behind
I thought I was looking cool

But the reality is I was looking bad
Because the inside was so sad. . . .
I plan to improve my self-esteem by remembering my grandma's
Words of wisdom and knowing that I am somebody
Self-esteem for me is tricky, some days I am high, others low
I want to get to a place where my self-esteem will stay high
Where I can feel good about myself and
Not give a damn about who likes it.

After she read her new rap, we spent most of the session speaking about the rap and discussing strategies for Yolanda to put her words into action. As a result of her rap, we were able to discuss the relationship of "putting things before" herself to her rap the week before of loving herself when she was with her daughter. Through this discussion, she was able to further internalize the value of loving herself independent of others. Our conversation included a discussion about her insight into wearing baggy clothes to hide behind "because the inside was so sad." Furthermore, we were able to discuss the dynamic normality of the ups and downs of self-esteem. Yolanda was happy to hear that her challenges with maintaining a high level of self-esteem were not uncommon. I was able to reinforce her desire to improve her self-esteem by reviewing some strategies she could use to improve it. For example, I asked her to write a list of ten positive things she liked about herself and techniques she could use to challenge negative self-defeating thoughts with positive self-affirming thoughts.

During our discussion, Yolanda reported that she was getting out of the house more often, interacting with friends, and maintaining her abstinence from marijuana. At the conclusion of the session, we listened to "Keep Your Head Up" by Tupac Shakur and I asked her to write a rap on how she planned to "keep her head up" in the following weeks.

The following week Yolanda came to her next appointment excited and ready to share and discuss her new rap. The following is an excerpt from what she read:

> *In times of fear I gotta keep my head up*
> *In times of turmoil I gotta keep my head up*
> *In times of weariness I gotta keep my head up. . . .*
> *In times of loneliness I gotta keep my head up*
> *In times of doubt I gotta keep my head up*
> *In times of prayer I gotta put my head down*
> *In time to receive my blessings*
> *I gotta keep my head up!*

Through the use of rap, Yolanda had begun to internalize and direct her recovery from depression and drug use. When asked what she meant by "in times of turmoil," she said she had to continue to be positive despite the stressful conditions around her. When asked what she meant by "in times of weariness," she responded, "Come on doc. You know I have to continue battling my negative thoughts." Rapping gave Yolanda a voice to articulate her challenges while finding her own solutions.

To help Yolanda resolve her difficult relationship with her grandmother, we listened to and discussed "I Miss You" by DMX, her favorite artist and who dedicated the rap to his grandmother. Yolanda was able to begin to speak about the love and appreciation she had for her grandmother. She was also able to develop some insight into the reasons why her grandmother did not want her to smoke marijuana. After not communicating with her grandmother for six months, Yolanda was finally able to visit her. As treatment progressed, Yolanda moved back into her grandmother's home and was able to find a part-time job at a local grocery store. Her symptoms of depression slowly abated. Her sleep and appetite improved. She was able to regain an active social life full of drug-free laughter. As we concluded our work together, I asked Yolanda to reevaluate her self-esteem. She rated it as being a 9.5 on the scale I gave her earlier (see Figure 2). She reported that she would have given herself a 10, but felt that there was always room for improvement.

Figure 2. Self-Esteem Rating

	CURRENT	GOAL
10		X
9	X	
8		
7		
6		
5		
4		
3		
2		
1		

Postscript

The case of Yolanda is interesting and has implications and similarities to many of the issues confronting urban youth. Yolanda reported "that she wears baggy clothes to hide behind" because she did not feel good about her body image. Not only can this be seen to be directly related to herself, but one could conceptualize this interpretation as generalizing the reasons why many urban youth wear baggy clothes.

16. THE CASE OF BRAD

BRAD IS a sixteen-year-old African American male who dropped out of high school at the beginning of his junior year after becoming involved with a local gang and selling drugs. He was referred to me through a worker who was doing outreach with local youth who had dropped out of school. Brad arrived at my office on time for his first appointment. He was casually dressed, clean cut, and appeared like a typical urban adolescent. He did not wear any jewelry.

Chief Complaint

When Brad came into my office, he was very polite. I asked him what I could do for him. He told me, "I'm trying to get my life together, I dropped out of school about two months ago and I think I need to get back up in there." I asked him how he got an appointment with me. He said, "Big Eddie B. set it up." He said, "Eddie B. was in the barbershop two weeks ago talking to me and a couple of my boys about health care and other shit like that." I asked him why Eddie B. was talking about health care in the barbershop.

He said, "You know Eddie B. is good people. He's always try-ing to get brothers to get their life back together. I see that brother everywhere, at the basketball court, the barbershop, the bus stop, the store, and just about everywhere else. Eddie B. is always talk-ing that positive shit. He always wants to know if we got health insurance, if we're still in school, if we're fucking with drugs, if we're eating good foods not just fried chicken and pizza. That's why I said Eddie B. is always talking that positive shit. He's a cool brother, I remember he used to be off the hook. My boys told me Eddie B. used to be banging and slanging but now that brother is righteous. Me and my boys got mad respect for big Eddie B. So Eddie B. told me I should come and see you and said that you could help me get my shit back together."

I asked Brad how he thought I could help him get his life back together. He said, "You could help a brother get back in school and leave some of these drugs alone." I told Brad I would be happy to help him and that I needed to get some more informa-tion from him. I also informed him that I would be taking some notes to get in his chart. So we began the intake procedure and I got some more biographical and demographic information from him.

History of Chief Complaint

Brad was raised by his mother and father in an urban com-munity. He reported that his father was physically abusive to him, his mother, and his younger brother and sister. His brother and sister are one and two years younger than him, respectively. He said that his mother was always loving to him and his brother and sister, but she never stood up to his father. He was insightful to the effects of the domestic violence on himself and his family and questioned his mother's loyalty to him and his brother and sister since she would not leave his father.

He reported that the primary reason he got involved with a gang and dropped out of school was because of the domestic violence. Several members of his gang lived in households with physically abusive fathers, so the gang was a strategy often used to gain a sense of security and safety. Unfortunately, the gang had other effects that compromised his behavior and decision making. He got involved with using drugs through the gang when he was fifteen. He was drinking alcohol, smoking cigarettes and marijuana, and sniffing cocaine.

He reported that he was very angry with his situation. He often thought about "putting his father in his place." He reported that he had moved out of his parents' house because he and his father got into a big fight after his father hit his mother and he began defending her. When the police came to his home, both parents said he started the fight with his father for no reason.

At the conclusion of our first session together, I encouraged Brad to see someone about his substance abuse issues. I referred him to a substance abuse treatment program and gave him the telephone numbers to several narcotics anonymous support groups in his neighborhood. We made an appointment for him to return to my office the following week.

Course of Treatment

The following week Brad arrived on time. I asked him if he had followed up with my referral for substance abuse treatment. He had not. Once again, I encouraged him to pursue treatment for substance abuse issues and gave him a list of resources in the community that could assist him.

Brad was wearing a Wu Wear jersey. I asked him if he liked Wu Wear. He replied, "No doubt, it's all about the wu baby, brothers like Ghost Faced Killer and Method Man represent my culture." I asked him what he meant by "my culture." He said emphatically, "Hip-hop culture, baby." So we began a discussion about hip-hop culture.

He said one of the reasons he dropped out of school was because he was learning more from hip-hop than he was from going to school. I asked him what he meant by that. He said that the real education took place in the back streets and alleys. He said all that stuff they teach in school is the same stuff he learned in the streets. He gave an example of how he learned more math by playing dice than by going to math class. He said he learned more in the streets than he learned in social studies. He said he learned more about sex education in the barbershop than he did in health class. He said he learned more about creative arts by listening to rap music and rapping than by going to English class. Furthermore, he said he got more insight from rap music than he got from reading literature. I asked him if he could give me an example of how he gained insight through rapping. He said, "Give me some paper and a pencil and I will give you some insight." He wrote the following:

> *Please don't push me chump ass niggaz*
> *Eyeing me, temp me*
> *Feeling lonely and unwanted makes me feel empty.*
> *Working on myself in treatment*
> *It's the first time in my life*
> *Finally seeing my life being dragged through strife. . . .*
> *I am seeing my shame*
> *Getting steamed and hot enough to spit flame.*

I asked him to provide me with the insight revealed in this rap. He reported that through writing raps he was able to get a lot of "shit" off his back and really take a look at some of the factors that made him behave the way he did. He reported that the first stanza indicated one of the reasons why he had a short fuse and oftentimes got into altercations and fights. He reported that because he was oftentimes feeling "lonely, unwanted, and empty," he would easily get threatened by people looking at him for extended periods of time. Furthermore, by coming to see me and thinking about some of the issues we had been discussing, he had become more aware of his "shame," which exacerbated his anger.

I told him he was right in many ways. His writing did provide him with a significant level of insight. I encouraged him to continue to write and rap and asked if he would like to use rap as a therapeutic tool in our work together. He thought that would be a good idea. Since he revealed his anger through rap, we were able to discuss some anger management strategies and relaxation techniques that he might find helpful when he found himself getting angry. I gave him some anger management material to read and think about until our next appointment. I asked him to think about some of the other things that made him angry and write about them for our next meeting together.

The following week I began by asking Brad if he had followed through with my recommendation to contact one of the substance abuse treatment programs about which I informed him. I was happy to learn that he had set up and followed through with an appointment at the substance abuse treatment program within the clinic I was working for at the time. I reinforced his motivation and encouraged him to continue to follow through as a means of accomplishing his goals.

We continued with Brad sharing the rap he had written following our last visit. He shared the following:

The illest Gangstaz raised me since I was young
Taught me how to cook and oh yeah
I got peoples from every scene
Ready to take away your means of cream.

The rap continued with ongoing angry lyrics but no true mention of the cause of his anger. We discussed the absence of the cause of his deep-rooted anger. He was unable to identify anything specific, other than his ongoing obsessive anger with his father for abusing his mother.

This insight allowed us to continue exploring his anger toward his father and how his father's anger appeared to be transferred to him. With time, Brad was able to realize that he had unconsciously internalized the vices he attributed to his father as virtues for himself. This was disturbing for Brad, since he did not want to emulate any aspects of his father, especially violent characteristics.

He became more determined than ever to rid himself of these internalized artifacts of his father's character. He was able to identify spirituality as a primary tool he wanted to utilize to rid himself of his predisposition toward his father's violence. A couple of weeks later, he wrote a rap about his use of spirituality to manage his anger. The following excerpt is from his rap:

The places I have lived, have turned me away from my righteous
God giving way
I am angry and I don't know why
When I would find myself angry in the past
I would oftentimes use my fist or physical tools to solve my problems. . . .
There is none greater than thee that I serve as my higher power
As I use my mind to solve problems
I find myself coming to grips with the only few people who enjoy
peace of mind and contentment in this day and time
Are the elect of God
Though they are persecuted from City to City

and falsely accused and denied the credit due them because of their
*   righteousness I find myself to be one of the few*
because I believe I don't have to be an asshole for you to see that I am
*   not pleased with your actions towards me*
my own self-pity is not a healthy way to deal with my anger
leave the guns the crack and knives alone
and pick up a pen and pad and I'm quick to grab a microphone
and make love to ear drum
I yell for attention
Beware of the fierce-some
Peace, Brad out.

We were able to discuss multiple themes from this new rap. We discussed the relationship and connection of his anger with violence and use of "physical tools" to resolve his anger. We discussed the continuum of anger and the multiple nonviolent outlets for anger. We discussed the concept of "peace of mind" and its dynamic nature. This led to a discussion about the use of relaxation techniques and other strategies for maintaining "peace of mind." We discussed his thoughts of "self-pity" contributing to his violent and angry outbursts. Finally, we discussed his ideas of substituting guns, drugs, and knives with a pen, paper, and a microphone. I reinforced his healthy use of writing rap music to help him manage his anger in a functional and productive way.

For the next three weeks, I continued to monitor his substance abuse treatment. As our relationship and treatment improved, his commitment to regain his sobriety continued to improve. We concluded our work with Brad writing about his plans to use different "support systems" to help him manage his anger. Brad wrote the following rap about the use of his support systems:

The support system I have is my family, they are my support
but my main support system is my one truth and living God
*   (Allah)*

*Allah, supports me in situations that no one will ever be able to help
    me with*
*Allah isn't only my main support system but he is also my mental
    guide as well. . . .*
*I need support around the issues of everyday life not just moment to
moment events turned bad*
I fear this world from what I have been through and heard. . . .
*If I didn't use the support from my brother and sister I would not
    know the first thing about love, sharing, and compassion. . . .*
I owe more to my family for their support of me.

I reinforced Brad's writing by providing him with positive reinforcement for his raps. At this point in treatment, Brad and I
had been working together for twelve weeks. He had seven
weeks of sobriety and was slowly transitioning out of his relationship with the gang. He reportedly did not engage in any more of
the "negative" activities and behaviors of the gang. He discontin-
ued treatment with me because he and his family decided it
would be beneficial for him to move "down South" and stay with
his cousins to continue his ongoing separation from the gang. I
was able to provide him with a list of counseling and substance
abuse treatment resources he could use once he relocated. Brad
was able to use rap music in a curative way. His progress in treatment was substantially improved and enhanced by his use of
writing rap music to communicate some of his goals, verbalize
some of his fears, and gain insight into some of the unconscious
dynamics that were having a significant impact on his behavior,
thoughts, and emotions.

17. THE CASE OF BOB

BOB WAS a thirteen-year-old Portuguese boy who lived in the inner city of a major northeastern city. His grandmother scheduled his first appointment with my office because of his "smart mouth." Bob arrived for his first visit with his grandmother and presented himself as a well-dressed, cooperative, and quiet boy. His grandmother was cooperative, supportive, and a bit eccentric in her dress and behavior.

Bob's grandmother had legal custody of her grandson and his older sister because of the sudden death of their mother due to illness. At the time of their mother's death, both children were being raised by their mother in a single-parent household. Bob had never met or spoken to his father. He was an athletic boy who spent most of his social time engaged in different sporting activities such as basketball, baseball, football, and snowboarding in the winter. His grandmother was very supportive of his athletic interests. When Bob was not playing sports, he enjoyed listening to rap music.

Bob was in relatively good health with the exception of several food allergies and seasonal hay fever. He got good grades in school and did not have a "smart mouth" at school. He did not normally get into trouble in school.

Chief Complaint

Bob's grandmother reported that her grandson had been verbally inappropriate with her because he frequently "talks back." She went on to report that he made "smart remarks" that were inappropriate. Interestingly, Bob's problems were reported to be limited to his interactions with his grandmother. The behavior began following the death of his mother. When Bob was asked how he felt about his grandmother's comments, he simply put his head down and said, "I don't know."

Course of Treatment

One of the most interesting presenting aspects of Bob was the dichotomy of the chief complaint and his interaction with me. He was reportedly an adolescent boy with a disrespectful and impulsive tongue. However, during each of his interactions with me, he presented himself as a quiet, depressed, and slightly withdrawn adolescent who was respectful and cooperative. His interests and hobbies appeared to be consistent with an adolescent boy in his age range living in an urban setting.

Since Bob presented himself as a quiet boy, we began our relationship by talking about things he found most interesting: his hobbies. Since he reported his hobbies included sports and rap music, I began developing a relationship with him by discussing these two topics. During our second meeting together, we talked about the sports he enjoyed playing; this got him to open up as he told me why he liked the sports.

The following week we began discussing his interest in rap music. Bob reported his favorite rap artists and songs were Ludacris's "Area Codes," Jay-Z's "Girls", and Cash Money's

"Project Chick." When asked why he liked these songs, he simply said he liked what they were saying and the "bling bling in the videos." He was able to recite the lyrics in full for each song. Considering Bob's loss of his mother (the primary woman in his life), I found it interesting that his three favorite songs were thematically related to the gender of his loss. This thematic interest could be interpreted as being his intense fantasy to replace his mother with poor "girls" throughout the country/ world who he felt he could control through some form of financial wealth. This theme is consistent with the portrayal of male-female relationships in many of the music videos watched by youth on television.

While discussing his interest in rap music, we looked through a *Source* magazine together and discussed different advertisements, articles, and music videos. The third week together we continued to discuss rap music and sports. As an attempt to merge his two favorite hobbies, which would allow him to become comfortable with writing about his interests, I asked Bob if he thought he could write a rap about his favorite athlete. He reluctantly agreed to write a rap about "The Answer" (Allen Iverson). He wrote the following excerpt:

> *A.I. Is my favorite basketball player*
> *His skills are rarer and rarer*
> *He J's in people's mouth*
>   *And he breaks their ankles*
> *That's why he is my favorite player*
>   *And he is a good team leader.*

After Bob finished writing his rap, he read it to me. I gave my customary positive reinforcement and we discussed the contents of his rap. The following week, we began discussing the issue that brought him to my office. As we listened to a Jay-Z tape he brought with him to my office, I asked what he thought about his grand-mother's reports that he had a smart mouth. The following conversation followed:

    Bob: She gets smart with me, so sometimes I say things.
    Dr. E: So are you suggesting that you do occasionally say things that you should not say to your grandmother.
    Bob: Yeah, when I get heated I talk back to her
    Dr. E: Can you think of ways that you could deal with your frustration differently, so that she does not think you are getting smart with her
    Bob: I don't know . . . I guess so.
    Dr. E: Do you think you can write a rap about it like the rap you wrote me last week on A.I.
    Bob: Hmm, I don't know about that.
    Dr. E: Why don't you give it a try.
    Bob: Alright.
    Dr. E: During the next week, I would like for you to work on the rap and we will discuss it when you come to my office next week.
    Bob: Okay.

The following week, Bob came to my office on time escorted by his grandmother. While his grandmother waited in the waiting room, Bob and I began our meeting with my customary inquiry about his week since the last time we saw one another. He reported that things were going well at home and school. He asked if he could turn on the radio in my office. I replied "sure" and asked if he had his assignment with him. He initially said he forgot to do it but eventually pulled a folded piece of paper out of his back pocket. He read the following:

I wrote about how I can handle situations with my grandmother by:
Keeping my mouth shut,
Doing what I am told, even if I don't like it
Or think that it fit
I can draw what I saw,
I could go play my games and get in the hall of fames
Or I can go outside and play ball with my friends.

I informed him that I thought he had done a great job writing a rap about how to improve his communication with his grandmother. We talked about the content of his rap and how he could enact some of the things about which he wrote.

For the following week, I asked Bob if he thought he could write a rap about how to improve his relationship with his grandmother and he reluctantly agreed. The following week he arrived at my office and read the following rap:

I can keep a good relationship with grandma
By doing what I am told
And doing good things for her
Doing the things that she ask me to do.
When she says something I don't like
I don't have to say anything
I can just smile and say it's a lil' thing.

Once again, I praised Bob for his insightful and creative expression. I told him that his raps could be considered his "action plan" for improving his relationship with his grandmother.

I then asked him, "What are some of the things that your grandma asks you to do that typically lead to an argument and of you becoming 'smart' with her?" He said, "When she tells me to do my homework or do some work around the house." So we discussed how he "could do what I am told" when she asked him to do the things that led to these verbal disagreements.

I then asked Bob if it would be okay to invite his grandmother into our session to discuss how much progress he had made and what his "plan of action" for improving his "smart mouth" was. He agreed.

When Bob's grandmother came in, we discussed his progress, his raps, and his action plan. He read his raps to his grandmother. She appeared surprised but somewhat skeptical of his commitment. I explained to her that these raps were an important step in the right direction and that it was important to give Bob the benefit of the doubt. She agreed.

I then asked her to give Bob and I a few minutes of privacy to wrap up our meeting. After her departure from my office, I debriefed with Bob about the exchange and his thoughts. He was very happy with the exchange and reported he was excited about putting his action plan to work. For the following week, I asked him to write a rap about how he could avoid getting angry with his grandmother when she asked him to do things he did not want to do. He said he would give it a try.

The following week, he arrived for his appointment early. He began the session by asking if I had seen a "step show" featured on 106th and Park (a rap video show on BET). I told him I had seen the final competition between the Kappas and the Sigmas (two black fraternities competing on the show). He reported that he thought the step show was exciting. We discussed how many black fraternities step (rap) in college. He said, "I gotta go to college." This interest was reinforced and discussed at some length during the remainder of our visit together.

I then asked Bob if he had written a rap for me. He said, "Oh yeah, I almost forgot." He read the following rap:

Today I am writing on how not to get angry with grandma
One, do what I am told,

Two, don't start anything
Three, don't get on punishment
Four, respect my grandma.

Once again, I provided Bob with positive reinforcement for his creativity and insight. We discussed the progression of his rap and how one through four were related and ultimately led to anger. Bob was able to realize that if he did not "get on" punishment, he would not get as angry and his anger would not be maintained for extended periods of time.

I asked Bob if there was anything that he and his grandmother did not agree on that contributed to ongoing arguments. He reported that they often disagreed about the length of his hair. I asked if he could write a rap about how he could avoid getting smart with his grandmother about the length of his hair. He said okay. The following week he read the following rap:

I think we can avoid arguments by letting me get braid
So that it looks neat
And I don't have to worry about picking it out
That makes sense,
And I don't even like my hair short.

We discussed his interest in having braids. His grandmother came into the session to discuss her concerns. She reported that she did not mind if he got braids but that she did not like for him to leave the house with his hair uncombed. They agreed that Bob could get braids if he made sure he kept the braids neat. Bob's use of writing raps as a form of expression continued to work in his relationship building with his grandmother.

Bob's grandmother reported she noticed a significant improvement in his behavior at home after several weeks of individual rap therapy. During our final week together, I told Bob that he should continue to review the raps he wrote for me about managing his relationship with his grandmother. I encouraged him to continue to use rap as a road map and action plan to maintain a good communication style with his grandmother. He agreed. For his final rap on maintaining a good relationship with his grandmother, he read the following:

> *I can keep a good relationship with my nanna*
> *By not getting smart*
> *Doing what I have to do*
> *Just to be good*
> *And doing what I am told.*

I reinforced his final rap. I asked him if he wanted to type the rap and print it out for his grandmother as a contract of his commitment to improving his relationship with her and getting rid of his "smart mouth." He agreed.

Postscript

A year later I contacted Bob's grandmother to find out how he was doing. She reported that their relationship had improved substantially and that he no longer spoke back to her in an inappropriate manner. However, she was becoming concerned about the friends he was hanging out with. She agreed that if things did not improve she would contact me . The case remains closed.

18. The Case of BarBara

BarBara was a twenty-six-year-old African American woman. She made an appointment for individual psychotherapy at the request of her substance abuse counselor. She had been in substance abuse counseling for four months. At the time of her first appointment with me, she had five months of sobriety. The referral from her substance abuse counselor indicated that she had a ten-year history of marijuana abuse, a six-year history of cocaine abuse, and a four-year history of substance abuse with Canadian Mist and Brandy. She was referred to me for individual therapy that focused on improving her self-esteem and self-worth that had been shattered during an eight-year verbally and physically abusive relationship with a man ten years her senior.

Chief Complaint

She arrived for her first visit well dressed, talkative, and open to discussion. She reported that her substance abuse counselor had referred her to my office to discuss issues related to her self-esteem and trauma history. She reported that her trauma history began eight years ago with verbal arguments, reprimands, and put-downs. The verbal abuse progressed into physical abuse one year later. The physical abuse climaxed three years later with the client smashing her boyfriend's head with a brick after he began pushing and hitting her with a skillet. The consequence of the latter incident was six months of probation. The client was remorseful of the incident and reported that she was working on anger management skills with her substance abuse counselor.

She reported that the abuse contributed to her low self-esteem and feelings of worthlessness. I asked her why she thought the abuse compromised her self-esteem. I asked her if she blamed herself for her victimization. She reported that she blamed herself for not leaving her boyfriend sooner and for allowing him to continue to verbally and physically abuse her. She reported that she did not blame herself for the physical or verbal abuse, but she did blame herself for not developing a plan or having the courage and confidence to leave the relationship sooner. She went on to say that her lack of initiative contributed to her feelings of worthlessness and reinforced her low self-esteem. Furthermore, she reported that she felt guilty that she allowed her daughter to witness the abuse and become the victim of verbal abuse herself.

I asked BarBara if she would be willing to complete a self-esteem assessment. As mentioned earlier, the self-esteem assessment simply allows people to rate from 1 (low) to 10 (high) how they currently perceive their self-esteem and what they hope it will be in the future. The client agreed to complete the scale. Her pretreatment rating of her self-esteem was a 5 and her goal was a 10 (see Figure 3). We would eventually return to the scale seven weeks later to determine if her self-esteem had improved.

Figure 3. Self-Esteem Rating

	CURRENT	GOAL
10		X
9		
8		
7		
6		
5	X	
4		
3		
2		
1		

History of Chief Complaint

BarBara's grandmother raised her in the inner city. She was the second of three children (all girls). She had a good relationship with her parents during her childhood, and her relationship with her siblings was very supportive and loving. Both of BarBara's sisters were also victims of verbal and physical abuse by their boyfriends. She did well in school until high school, when she began using drugs. Her drug use began with cigarettes and eventually progressed to alcohol and experimentation with illicit drugs. She had a limited work history as a receptionist at a community center. She was currently on welfare and lived with her mother and daughter.

Hobbies

Her hobbies included dancing, singing, spending time with her family, and watching television. She enjoyed dancing and singing to a variety of urban music and jazz. I asked her if she had ever written any music of her own. She responded, "No, but I think I could write a few blues songs given what I've been through." I asked her if she would be willing to write a few songs during our work together. She said, "I've never had to write a song for a psychologist before. If it helps, I'm all for it." We concluded a first session and met again a week later.

Course of Treatment

The following week she arrived on time and continued to disclose some background information. We continued to work on improving our relationship. At the end of the session, I asked her if she could write me a song about self-love. She responded by saying, "Sure, I'll give it a try." The following week she arrived and read the following song:

> *to be young gifted and black*
> *that's a fact*
> *I will take my life back*

to be young gifted and black
I will take no slack
to be young gifted and black
that's where I'm at!!

I told her that I was amazed by her ability to write such a beautiful song. I asked how her song related to her self-love. BarBara responded by saying, "This song was very difficult to write because I usually don't think about myself in a positive way." I asked her if there was a particular song or artist that she thought about while working on this song. To my surprise, she reported that she was thinking of Mariah Carey's "Butterfly." She went on to say that she was a big Mariah fan and one of the reasons that she enjoyed listening to Mariah's music and watching her videos was because she thought that Mariah was an empowered woman who was very attractive and very talented. These were many of the qualities she dreamed of developing in herself.

I told her that I was not familiar with Mariah's song "Butterfly" and asked if she could tell me a little bit about the song and how it related to the song that she wrote. BarBara informed me that "Butterfly" was the title of the CD as well as of her favorite song on the CD. She went on to say that one of the reasons she liked the song so much was because she thought that it described how she could develop into a beautiful butterfly as long as she maintained hope, faith, determination, and prayer. I asked her what exactly did she mean. She said she believed that she had a little butterfly inside of her that had been imprisoned by her abusive history, self-doubt, and depression. She went on to say that by maintaining hope for the future she gave the butterfly inside her the opportunity to grow, by keeping faith she could hold onto her dreams, and by having determination she could maintain the hard work required to let the butterfly continue to develop and grow. Through prayer, she believed she would be guided in the right direction to let her butterfly reach its full potential.

I thought it was interesting that she had such a well thought out plan and yet she continued to suffer from self-doubt and depression. So I asked her if this was something that she often thought about or if she thought about this as a result of the exercise I asked her to write earlier in the week. She said that through the exercise she was able to think about why she really liked this song and how the song related to her life. Through the exercise she was able to develop some insight into a repressed goal that she had never acknowledged consciously.

> *In order to improve self-esteem*
> *you need to be positive*
> *you need to look ahead to your future*
> *without self-esteem there is self-doubt.*
> *In order to keep your self-esteem*
> *you might need to screem, pout, or shout.*
> *But whatever you do*
> *believe in you*
> *keep your head high*
> *and your self-esteem will start to glean*
> *self-esteem itself is self-worth*
> *without it you can't go forth.*

I told BarBara that that was a beautiful piece of writing. I asked her if she could explain how it related to Mariah's "Butterfly." She said, "I told you. The butterfly is me and I'm trying to develop into all I can be. It ain't easy, but with hope, and like I said prayer I can do anything." I asked her if she found the exercise helpful. She said the exercise was very helpful because it allowed her to think about her dreams, hopes, and fears and how they were all related to her low self-esteem.

I told her that another value of what she wrote and how she had conceptualized what she wrote was that it gave her a road map to follow and develop her "butterfly." I told her that she may want to consider writing down her four points and review them each day. By maintaining hope, faith, determination, and prayer, she would be able to develop into a beautiful butterfly. I asked her what other songs or artists gave her inspiration. She said, "Surprising as it may seem, I love Tupac." Since it was time for our session to end, I told her to think about her favorite Tupac Shakur song and write a rap about how it related to her self-esteem. I asked her to bring it in with her the following week and share it with me.

Since she was so insightful and immediately took to the exercises of using music in a therapeutic way, I thought that I would give her an opportunity to continue developing her own blueprint for her treatment. I was hopeful that she would continue to move in a positive direction. However, I was uncertain what she would produce for the following week.

The following week BarBara arrived on time and in a very pleasant mood. I began by asking her if she had completed her assignment. She said yes and read the following rap:

keep your head up
I have to keep my head up
keeping your head up
means being proud of who you are today
never letting the past get in the way
sometimes the road might sway
but remember you have to pay to play
now that I paid there is no room for play
I have lost too many things along the way
I no longer want to play
with my life
I have found a new way.

After reading the rap, she said, "I guess you know what Tupac song is my favorite." I said, "Let me take a guess: 'Keep Your Head Up.' " She said, "That's right, if we are talking about self-esteem, then I have to keep my head up." She went on to say, "Tupac is one of my favorite artists. I could relate to him when he talked about all the different aspects of life from the good to the bad." So I asked her if the rap she wrote described how she planned to keep her head up and if keeping her head up was part of her plan for improving her self-esteem. She said, "Yeah, I have to keep my head up and not let the past events get me down."

I reviewed with her several strategies she could use to improve her self-esteem. We discussed the power of having a positive outlook on life and developing more optimistic views. I asked her if she could list ten things she liked about herself. I was surprised to find out that despite writing such positive rap, she was only able to list three things that she liked about herself. She reported that she liked the fact that she was a mother, that she was sober, and that she was no longer in a physically abusive relationship. I listed another five positive attributes and questioned her as to why I was able to name more positive attributes about her than she was. She simply shrugged her shoulders. I asked her if she agreed with any of the attributes that I listed and she agreed with all of them. She went on to say that she believed that since she had been in so many negative relationships in which her partner spoke down to her that she found it very difficult to identify positive attributes about herself. She said, "Now if you ask me about some negative attributes, I could give you at least twenty." I reminded her that the purpose of our work together was to increase the number of positive attributes she could identify about herself, not reinforce the negative attributes that she continued to identify.

I suggested that she begin tracking her negative thoughts about herself so that she could begin to challenge them with positive alternative thoughts. I provided her with a form that had three columns, the first column was the date, the second column was titled "Negative Thoughts," and the third column was titled "Positive Alternatives." Her assignment was to identify and track each negative self-thought and come up with an alternative thought that was positive. The exercise would allow us to identify the frequency of her negative thoughts and common themes of her negative thoughts. Furthermore, the chart would allow her to begin developing positive alternative thoughts as substitutes for her negative thoughts. I informed her that it was important to follow through with this assignment each day for the next three weeks and that we would review it at each of our sessions together. This exercise would run concurrently with our ongoing rap therapy.

When BarBara arrived the following week, I suggested that we listen to "Video" by India Arie. I suggested that while listening to the song she should think about how it related to the value of identifying positive aspects about herself. We listened to the song together and then discussed how the song related to her. She found the song to be very uplifting. She said that by listening to the song and thinking about the list of the positive attributes I used to describe her the previous week that she finally realized how she was taking the positive attributes about herself for granted. She said, "I need to recognize the positive aspects about myself just like I recognize the negative aspects." For the following week, I asked her to write a rap about some of the things that she liked about herself.

The following week she arrived with both her chart and her rap. She said, "Let's start with my little rap." She read the following:

I am a powerful black woman today
I know I have choices and I don't have to settle for less

I am a woman of worth
I am a woman of dignity
I am a woman who can accomplish anything
now that I have my head out of the clouds
I am a woman with her feet on solid ground
I am a woman who is intelligent, creative, loving, and
    a great parent.

As with each of her earlier raps, I gave her positive reinforcement for her new rap. She went on to say that each of the references about herself in the rap came from the chart that she was using to track her negative thoughts. She had written on her chart that she was worthless and unable to complete anything. So she incorporated the alternative way of conceptualizing these negative thoughts as positive thoughts into her rap. She went on to say that the exercise was helping her catch herself before making negative comments.

We then talked about how her self-concept was closely linked to her relationships with men. I told her that I believed that her substance abuse and low self-esteem were all related to her difficulties in intimate relationships. With this in mind, it was important for her to begin to think about how she would not let relationships make her relapse with drugs and low self-esteem. For the following week, I asked her to continue working on her chart and to write a rap about how she could prevent herself from relapsing in her next relationship. The following week she shared the following rap:

when in a relationship never lose sight of who you are
or you won't go far
I must tell my partner what I want
and don't let them pull a stunt
I must set goals for myself

I must not compromise my physical well-being
I must not compromise my chance to further my education or my
        dreams
I must make sure my partner knows
where I want to be in the future
how I want to raise my children
and how I plan to reach my goals.
If he loves me
he will stay with me
and get with the program.

After giving her positive reinforcement for this rap, I asked her how difficult she thought it would be to behave the way that she wrote about in an actual relationship. Surprisingly, she said that she did not think it would be that difficult. She said, "Now that I have this shit written down, it's time for me to follow it through. You mark my motherfucking word Dr. Elligan. I don't mean to curse but I am on a mission." I asked her how she planned to stay out of verbally and physically abusive relationships. She said, "The same way I am going to stay away from drugs: avoid the people, places, and things." I asked her if she thought relapsing into a codependent relationship was just as easy as relapsing back into substance abuse. Surprisingly, she thought that relapsing into an abusive relationship was going to be easier than relapsing back into drug use. However, she was determined to avoid all intimate relationships until she felt better about her self-esteem and self-worth. I provided her with positive reinforcement for this new goal.

We continued to work on building her self-esteem for the next three weeks. During this time, we talked about other issues related to racism, sexism, work, housing, finances, and other concrete issues that are known to lead to relapse. Prior to our last session together, I asked her to write a rap about what she had gained through our work together. The following week she presented this rap:

> *I have learned how to keep it real*
> *and how good it feels*
> *when a sister makes no deals*
> *with how she feels*
> *I've learned that I am the pilot of mind*
> *I won't become the victim of a crack dealer's line*
> *all the worthlessness, self-doubt, self-pity, and fear*
> *has been left far behind*
> *I am keeping my head up and reaching for the stars.*

I told her that it was very important that she keep all of her writings and refer to them frequently for support and encouragement. I reinforced her belief that her writings were her road map for self-actualizing her goals. During our final session, I asked her to complete a self-esteem scale to determine if her self-esteem had improved during our work together. Before we began the treatment, she rated her self-esteem as a 5. During our last session together, she rated it as a 10 out of 10 on the same scale (see Figure 4). She had obviously seen significant improvement in her self-esteem.

Figure 4. Self-Esteem Rating

	CURRENT	GOAL
10	X	X
9		
8		
7		
6		
5		
4		
3		
2		
1		

19. THE CASE OF AMY

AMY WAS a twenty-seven-year-old European American of Irish descent who was referred to my office by a battered woman shelter. She arrived for her appointment on time and casually dressed in hip-hop clothing. She wore a pair of Timberland boots with baggy black pants and a red Phat Farm jersey. Her hair was braided in cornrows with several beads randomly arranged throughout. She was very easy to speak with and described herself as an upbeat extrovert who loved people.

Chief Complaint

When asked what brought her into my office, she replied, "I got relationship issues." When I asked what she meant by this, she said that she had been in several physically and verbally abusive relationships that always ended in separation. She was particularly concerned because she was currently separated from the father of her two daughters. She could recall five relationships that had ended due to physical abuse and thought it was time to put an end to the cycle.

History of Chief Complaint

Amy was raised with her younger sister by both of her parents in an abusive home. She reported that both of her parents were alcoholics while she was a child. Her father reportedly abused all of the women in the house. Throughout their adolescence, their father had molested both Amy and her sister. Amy denied that the molestation took the form of incest but reported that it included inappropriate touching and fondling. She never told her mother of the molestation until two years prior because she did not want to cause any more discord within the family, discord that could have resulted in further physical abuse. Her mother and father were currently divorced. She reported that once she and her sister graduated from high school, her mother divorced her father and moved out of state. Her father was currently living alone with multiple health problems. She said that no one in the family spoke to him and that he was a "lonely old man." In spite of her father, she continued to have a supportive relationship with her mother and sister.

While still in high school, Amy was very social but silently depressed. She said that she had never been seen by a counselor or mental health professional but thought it was time for her to see a professional. She confirmed that a social worker at the battered women's shelter referred her to my office. She had two daughters with the same man and had never been married. She was currently unemployed and had never held a steady job. She had a work history in the area of telemarketing.

I referred Amy to another clinic specializing in treating survivors of physical and sexual abuse. We continued to work on helping her improve her ability to develop healthy relationships.

Hobbies

In describing her hobbies, she reported that she enjoyed hanging out at clubs, dancing, and having a few drinks. She reported that she only liked rhythm and blues and hip-hop/rap music. She discussed at length how she would spend many of her afternoons watching rap videos to learn all the latest dance moves. She used the analogy of watching rap music videos like many women watch aerobic videos. She reported that it was nothing like the "high" of walking in a "club and having all the brothers want to get with you because you look different but can dance and dress like everybody else."

Course of Treatment

Amy had some insight into the potential historical connection of her current difficulty with relationships and her developmental relationship with her father. When I asked if the men she had dated in the past had anything in common, she reported that they had several things in common. "I like brothers, I only kick it with black men. I have always liked black men because they give me so much attention. As you can tell, I am a little heavier than those model-type white women, but the brothers love my weight. I only hang out in the black community because I am exotic here." She went on to speak about how she only hung out at black clubs and bars because that was where she got the most attention. She reported that white men did not find her attractive because they only liked "anorexic white girls."

Given her interest in rap music and hip-hop culture, I thought that it would be ideal to use rap music in our therapeutic work together. She was open to this idea and told me that she could probably teach me a thing or two about hip-hop. I told her that would be great and that maybe I could help her figure out why she oftentimes seemed to find herself in abusive relationships.

During our third meeting with one another, I asked her what she thought were some of the factors that contributed to her being attracted to abusive relationships. She was only able to identify her abusive relationship with her father as a potential cause. Through our discussions, she was able to gain some insight into how she oftentimes would "lose" her self-identity while in relationships and was unable to end relationships until after several repeated episodes of physical abuse.

Since she enjoyed listening to rap music, I suggested that we listen to "Unfoolish" by Ashanti (a rap song that discusses a woman leaving an unhealthy relationship) together and discuss any similarities the message in the song had with her difficulty in ending unhealthy relationships. She thought the song was empowering to listen to and discuss. She reported that she had never really listened to the lyrics critically or deconstructed the message of the song. She believed the song was relevant to her situation because of her difficulty in ending abusive relationships. I suggested that she continue to think about the song over the course of the next week and write a rap about how she thought she could maintain her self-respect in relationships. The following week she arrived for her appointment on time and read the following excerpt from her rap:

I can honestly say that I do not know how to be in a relationship
    without losing myself
Relationships with men have always been a downfall for me
A lot of it goes back to my relationship with my father
I seem to pick men who can only give me themselves for a while
They then leave me

From what I've been told I tend to attract people who can't lift me
      up emotionally or spiritually
I have settled for less
I am only able to see this right now
      and I'm trying to work on this issue a lot.

Having provided her with positive reinforcement for her rap, we began to deconstruct and discuss its meaning. I asked her why she thought that men could only give themselves to her temporarily. She said, "It's all good at first, that honeymoon phase, but then the shit starts to fall apart. I guess it's just that I don't know how to choose men or I choose them for all the wrong reasons." I asked, "What are the wrong reasons?" She replied, "The way they look, the type of ride they got, if they buy me drinks, if they make me laugh." We discussed how relationships built on some of those factors would have a difficult time lasting and continue to be healthy. I suggested that since her interest in relationships appeared to be a bit more long term, she might consider placing greater value on some long-term factors, such as personality or character, as opposed to if the person bought her a drink or drove a nice car. I suggested that she use the next week to extend her current rap about relationships to include a comment on her relationship with herself. The following week she returned with the following addition to her rap:

As far as my relationship with myself
I have just realized that I deserve a better life
This has been hard for me because
I have been afraid of the responsibility that comes with me trying to
      achieve my own goals
I have not let others be part of my life that can be there for me. . . .
My children give me hope
I want to teach them and show them that life is possible and that we can
      overcome the obstacles of life without losing self-respect.

This rap became a turning point in our treatment because Amy had begun to identify that she was worthy and deserving of having healthy relationships. She was able to identify another factor that contributed to her difficulty in having healthy relationships other than the trauma history with her father. She was also able to recognize how she had been "afraid" of taking responsibility for her life, which contributed to her settling for unhealthy relationships based on materialism. Furthermore, we were able to begin using her hope for her children to further strengthen her resolve to improve the relationships to which she exposed them. Through our discussion, Amy began to develop some insight into the connection that the settings in which she met men and how she presented herself in those settings were related to the type of men with which she would develop relationships.

She reported that her relationships with men were all about appearance and that men liked her because she looked "exotic," wore all the right clothes, and could hook up her makeup. I asked her if she was familiar with India Arie's song "Video." She was familiar was the song and said she liked India Arie's CD. I suggested that we listen to the song together and that she think about the meaning of the song in relationship to how her appearance was related to how she felt and thought about herself.

We listened to the song together and discussed the meaning afterward. She reported that she had never really paid attention to the lyrics of the song but thought it made a lot of sense. She said, "I need to work on loving me for me not for who I can dress up to be." For the following week, I encouraged her to continue to think about the lyrics of the song, the connection the lyrics had to her relationship with men, and to write a rap about how her self-image was related to her relationship difficulties.

The following week she arrived with her homework assignment and read the following piece from her rap?

The feelings I have about self-love
I really did not expect from above
I have had many days that I did not know about myself
When I just felt like there was no help
As I try to get it together and learn about myself and loving myself
I know that God will help me from above.

In discussing her rap, she said she realized that her need for acceptance and approval was multilayered. She realized that she would dress and behave a certain way so that men would recognize her, approach her, flirt with her, and buy her things, all so that she would feel good about herself momentarily. She went on to discuss how she had begun to realize that she used sex to maintain her relationships with men so that they would continue to buy her things that made her feel valuable. As we continued our discussion, I suggested that she might want to continue to think about how sex contributed to some of the relationship difficulties she had been having. I encouraged her to write a rap about any insights she developed. The following week she read this excerpt from the rap she had written:

I know that I have used sex for things and to help me deal with pain
I have always seen sex as a weapon
I always thought that sex meant love
I was sadly mistaken because mostly sex only brought
Pain and anguish for a moment of acceptance.

I asked Amy what she meant by "sex as a weapon." She said that she would use sex to get things she wanted. When men would abuse her, she would become fearful that they were going to leave her, so she would use sex to maintain the relationship. Sex became a weapon for maintaining what she was fearful of losing. I asked her why she thought that "sex only brought pain and anguish." She suggested that by using sex and maintaining the re-lationship, she simply perpetuated the abuse because the men would not leave but ultimately they would abuse her again. I asked her if she thought she could change this destructive cycle and she was convinced that she could. I asked her if she could outline her strategy to avoid getting into abusive relationships in the future. She came up with the following list:

1. Avoid men in nightclubs.
2. Don't place too much value on men flirting with me.
3. Focus on feeling good about myself independent of men.
4. Develop hobbies that make me feel good about myself.
5. Don't use sex as a weapon to keep men.
6. Don't tolerate any form of abuse.
7. Continue working with my trauma group.
8. Work on feeling good about myself without getting all dressed up for men.

I told her that I thought it was a good list of strategies she could use to help her avoid abusive relationships in the future. I asked her if there was any meaning to the order and she said no. She fur-ther suggested that after writing the list she realized that if she were to put one of the items at the top as the single most impor-tant issue, it would be number 6—not to tolerate any form of abuse.

For the next couple of weeks, we continued to discuss strate-gies she could use to avoid getting into negative and abusive rela-tionships. We spent some time role-playing on how she could speak with men without relapsing into her old patterns of com-munication. During our twelfth week, I suggested that she write a rap about self-esteem. The next week she read the following ex-cerpt from a rap she had written:

My view of self-esteem is that it is a feeling that comes from inside
How you respect, care, and love yourself.
A lot of people especially women do not have high self-esteem.
I do not have high self-esteem.
It is something I have not valued because of the home I grew up in.
I was not shown how to develop high self-esteem because I had poor
    role models. . . .
I believe my self-esteem is getting a little better
I'm not putting myself in questionable situations
I have been trying to build my self-esteem by coming to therapy,
talking about my issues, and working in my trauma group.

I reinforced Amy's belief that her self-esteem was improving and confirmed my belief that she had grown substantially since our first meeting. During the fourteen weeks we worked together, she was able to maintain a life without being physically abused. She reported that by using rap music in our sessions, she found it to be a positive learning resource and very valuable because rap music was her primary teacher. She reported that she would learn from rap videos how to dance, what type of clothes to wear, how to speak, and how to behave. She was happy to see that although rap music had reinforced a lot of negative messages she received from her family as a child, it was also just as powerful in helping her learn constructive coping skills to challenge and alter some of her dysfunctional thoughts and behaviors.

Postscript

Amy decreased the frequency of her visits with me over the next three months to one visit per month. During that period, she reported that she had not gotten into any abusive relationships.

For the first time as an adult, she was able to remain single for over four months. She began spending more time with her daughters and her mother and sister. She continued meeting regularly with her trauma group.

20. THE CASE OF THE LOST SIBLING

ARMANDO WAS a twelve-year-old Puerto Rican boy who was depressed from the sudden murder of his older brother. Prior to his brother's death, Armando was a social boy who oftentimes got in trouble at school for being very talkative and occasionally disruptive in class. His teacher suggested that the mother have him see a professional because she noticed a significant change in his behavior following his brother's death.

Chief Complaint

Following his brother's death, Armando's behavior at school displayed the following symptoms: he became extremely quiet, socially withdrawn, and would oftentimes put his head down on his desk and stare out the window. His mother reported that while at home he spent most of his time in his bed listening to music. His appetite had decreased significantly but he had not lost any weight. He also displayed symptoms of insomnia. He would not discuss his brother's death with anyone. He attended family grief counseling with his mother and father for two months;

however, he was never vocal in the meetings. His parents believed that he should be able to speak about his brother's death in one way or another to begin the healing process. They believed that his symptoms in school were directly related to his brother's death. Armando did not have any other siblings. He was close with several cousins that were in his age range. However, he withdrew from them after his brother's death.

History of Chief Complaint

During our first meeting, Armando's mother provided me with a bit of family background information while Armando quietly sat in my office. She reported that his brother had been shot during an argument in the park about the score of a basketball game.

Armando was born in Puerto Rico and moved with his family to a city in New England when he was six months old. His parents had moved to New England for work-related issues. Armando and his parents were fluent in English and all of our work together took place in English without the assistance of an interpreter. Armando did not speak voluntarily during the first meeting with the exception of his response to his limited discourse following the death of his brother. When his mother mentioned this, he replied, "I just don't like to think about it." Even so, his mother suggested that he spent most of his time thinking about his brother's death.

Hobbies

During the next couple of weeks, Armando and I spent time getting to know one another. We played card games and talked about his hobbies, which included playing video games and listening to rap music. His favorite rappers were Big Pun, Notorious B.I.G., and Tupac Shakur. I believed it was symbolically relevant that each of the three rappers he described as his favorite were deceased. He did not have any insight into the relationship of his favorite rappers and his brother. His favorite rap CD was *Life After Death* by Notorious B.I.G. At the conclusion of our third week together, I asked Armando if he would be willing to bring in his favorite rap CD to our next meeting together and he agreed.

Course of Treatment

The following week Armando arrived with his CD. I asked him to play his favorite song on the CD. He put the CD in the stereo and asked if we could play a game of UNO. We began playing UNO and listened to his favorite song "I'll Be Missing You," a tribute by Puff Daddy and Faith Evans to Notorious B.I.G. I mentioned that he did not tell me that Puff Daddy was one of his favorite artists. He replied that he just liked the song because it was about Notorious B.I.G. and it reminded him of his brother. This was significant because it was the first time that he had mentioned his brother in any context to me. As we continued to play cards, I asked why it reminded him of his brother. He replied, "Because I miss him, the song reminds me of him."

I then asked if he ever listened to the song with his parents and he said he had not because they didn't like rap music. I asked him if he would be willing to let his mother come in from the waiting room and listen to the song with us and see what she thought. He indicated that that would be fine but that she would not want to listen to any rap music. I went to the waiting room and informed his mother of our breakthrough and asked if she would be willing to come in and listen to the song with us and discuss it with Armando on their way home. She was happy to participate.

With all three of us sitting in my office, we listened to the song together and Armando's mother joined in our game of UNO. Surprisingly, half way through the song Armando began to cry and hugged his mother; she immediately began to cry as well. I asked if I should turn off the song and they both said "no." At the end of the song, Armando's mother said that it was a beautiful song and told Armando that they should listen to it together with his father that night. He went on to tell her that he liked the song because it reminded him of his brother. We spent some time talking about the grief process. Armando was able to inform his mother that even though he did not talk about the loss of his brother, he was always thinking about him. I suggested that it appeared that he had been grieving in silence, which was fine. I asked if he thought it would be okay to listen to the song with his father as his mother had suggested. He said that would be fine. I told him he could bring the CD back next week if he liked.

The following week Armando returned with his CD and we listened to it just as we did the week before. As we listened to his music, I asked him if he had ever written a rap about his brother. He said he could not write rap. I asked him if he would be willing to write a rap about his brother if I wrote a rap about my family. He agreed and we both tried to write something. After fifteen minutes, he was unable to write anything and asked if he could hear what I wrote. I shared the following with him:

My family is in unity
Promoting peace in the community
Making the hood a place of beauty
So all can walk in peace
And not worry about getting shot with a glock.

He laughed and said, "That's hype, I hope nobody else gets shot in my hood." We discussed the rap for about ten minutes and I suggested that he give writing a rap another try. After five minutes he was still unable to write anything. I told him that was fine and that we could try doing some writing the next time we got together.

The following week Armando arrived with the same CD. "I'll Be Missing You" had become the theme song for our work together. Furthermore, with the passing of each week Armando was slowly beginning to speak more and more about his brother's death. While listening to the song, he suggested that we both try to write a rap again. I agreed and we spent about eight minutes writing. He wrote and read the following short rap:

> *Dr. E. gave rap, right*
> *But can he step into the light*
> *And keep his rap tight.*

We both laughed at the rap. I told him I thought his rap was really good and he smiled. We continued to talk about his rap and other school-related issues. He was beginning to become more talkative in school and returning to his previous baseline of social interaction. He was able to openly speak about the loss of his brother with his family, teacher, and myself.

The following week we continued as we did in weeks past. During the time we spent writing together, he wrote the following rap titled "Brother":

> *It was a sad day in August*
> *He didn't have a long life*
> *But he was honest*
> *He would wrestle with me,*
>   *Sometimes drop me,*

But I always knew he cared for me.
He was my brother

I told him I thought the rap was beautiful. He said that it was the first time he was able to write about his brother. We discussed how it might be helpful for him to keep nice memories of his brother in a journal as a memorial. He thought it would be a good idea to start with this rap. I asked him if he wanted to write the rap on my computer and print it out to put in a folder or frame and hang it in a special place at home. He thought it would be nice to frame. He wrote the rap, printed it on yellow paper, cut it out, and framed it in an old frame in my office. He was very happy and pleased with his production. His mother provided further reinforcement as she picked him up from my office.

Armando and I continued to work together for the remainder of the academic school year. Our work together lasted a total of eight months until the end of the semester. He continued to grieve the loss of his brother. In school, he returned to being an energetic and social sixth grader. Constructive and therapeutic use of rap music had provided him with a medium for grieving that traditional family grief work was unable to accomplish alone. The use of rap music in the therapeutic process was consistent with Armando's pretreatment approach to grieving. Rap therapy provided him with an open, safe, and structured setting to continue the development of his grieving strategy.

21. THE SAFE-SEX GROUP

A LOCAL public high school requested that I facilitate a three-week course on the value of safe sex to a group of sophomore boys. The school was located in an inner-city section of a major metropolitan public school in New England. Students at the school were primarily of African American, Caribbean, and European American descent. Over the past five years, the school had a significant increase in the number of teenage pregnancies and invested a substantial amount of money in day care for the children of the students to help the students remain enrolled in school. Given the recent increase in the incidence of HIV infection among urban girls and young women, the focus of the group was on HIV education and prevention.

The Group

The group was composed of seven sophomore boys. The boys had volunteered to participate in the group and act as peer advocates for safe sex following participation in the group. The group met once a week for three weeks. The group began with a brief overview and introductions. Each of the boys knew one another. During our first meeting, we also discussed the influence of rap music and hip-hop on their lives. Each of the boys reported that rap music had a significant influence on him. After discussing rap music, I informed the students that we would use rap music in our sessions to facilitate the discussions about the value of safe sex and HIV education and prevention. Each of the boys was open to the idea.

During our first meeting together, we listened to a public service announcement (PSA) by Salt 'N' Pepa titled "I've Got AIDS" from the *Very Necessary* CD. The PSA is a dramatic skit between a girl and boy who have been intimate in the past and the girl just found out that she is HIV positive. After listening to the skit, the boys discussed their reactions and thoughts. The reactions ranged from shock to laughter. Each of the boys thought the skit was very realistic and disclosed similar situations with which friends had reportedly been confronted. We discussed how the use of condoms and other barrier prophylactics could have led to a different outcome. Each of the boys was to come back to group the following week with concrete strategies the couple could have used to avoid the outcome.

The following week the boys presented the following alternative behaviors:

1. Use a male condom.
2. Use a female condom.
3. Abstinence while dating.
4. Abstinence while fondling.
5. Abstinence while kissing.
6. Masturbation.
7. Oral sex.

We discussed the risk of each of the suggestions the boys reported. The conversation was engaging, informative, and supportive. After discussing the latter four suggestions, I gave the boys a handout from the Department of Public Health outlining safe sex and HIV-prevention behaviors. We also discussed the value of assertiveness and self-worth as integral parts of empowering oneself to take responsibility for engaging in sexually safe behaviors. We role-played different scenarios that required one to be assertive and empowered to maintain safe behaviors. We then listened to "Shorty Was Da Bomb" by DMX from his *Great Depression* CD. After listening to the song, the group discussed the implications the song had for safe sex.

The boys were very engaged in the discussion and brought up very interesting points. Their teachers were surprised to find out how involved and participatory each boy was without being disruptive. This is believed to be a function of the use of rap music as a teaching tool that is developmentally and culturally appropriate. At the end of the meeting, each member of the group was to do the following homework assignment. They were to write a rap about the importance of safe sex or HIV prevention.

The following week each of the boys came to the final group. Several boys had not done the assignment and the other members of the group gave them a hard time for it. One of the raps that was written was titled "Safe Sex":

If you're involved with any sexual activities
Let me hit you off with a taste of a melody

First thing first, pull out the rubber
Lay it on the table and say, "please don't tell my mother"
Some people think it's dumber and dumber
But while they're doing it they will say
It's funner and funner

When I was at my first WCW wrestling match I saw my boy Lex
And said what's the update on safe sex
Put the rubber on your penis
And say to the girl, baby I mean this
You can't catch HIV,
but if you don't want to do this just tell me and we'll let that be.

For all the females rockin' the lovely braids
Just because you're pretty and all, look out for the AIDS
From the brothers with the baldeys, braids and high-top fades

V.D.—venereal disease
It won't kill you, but it might give you herpes

In conclusion
The resolution
Of the pollution
Done to the Females and Males
Don't take this as fairy tales
Peace,
I'm Gone

After the student read his rap, the group applauded and provided him with positive reinforcement. We then had an interesting discussion about the content of his rap. Since the members were to become peer advocates, we discussed how the rap incorporated discussions about safe sex with friends. The student who wrote the rap further discussed how sexually transmitted diseases are often camouflaged by one's beauty as he said in the rap:

For all the females rockin' the lovely braids
Just because you're pretty and all, look out for the AIDS
From the brothers with the baldeys, braids and high-top fades

Furthermore, we discussed how the rap included a discussion about being assertive and respectful in the use of condoms. Each member of the group that completed a rap had an opportunity to read his work. The following is another original rap one of the students read entitled "Practice Safe Sex—A Male's Perspective":

Lady's and Gents
Children of all ages
Be cautious of AIDS. It comes
first two different stages
first to HIV, human immunodeficiency virus
sexually transmitted to the human body
once the disease erects in the immune system, it's vital
Which will limit the days toward your survival
having sex unprotected, it's really suicidal
fellah's think first before you crawl
Under the shirt control your hormones
Before you fill the urge to jerk
Yourself and situation far much worst
six months later you discover you
Got HIV, looking for a treatment to
Slow down the process of HIV
You should have remained abstinent
Or used protection, now you won't be able to
To have sex with another human being
Ever again, since the plague is
Spreading under your skin
Your life is now coming to an end.

After the student read his rap, everyone applauded and told him they really liked his rap. The student discussed the content of the rap. He reported that he found the writing to be helpful in contributing to his determination to be actively involved in the peer educator role of the project.

With the use of rap music, each of the students became actively involved and readily participated in the project. For many of the students, their level of involvement eclipsed that of their baseline participation in other classes.

Postscript

The administrators and teachers at the school found the group to be very instrumental in contributing to the development of the peer educator program they were developing. The students reportedly continued to be involved in the peer educator program through the conclusion of the academic year.

22. A Case of Sudden Loss to HIV and AIDS

Eric is the clinical case study of an eleven-year-old African American boy whose mother died of AIDS during the summer preceding his entrance into sixth grade. Eric did not know his father. It was believed that he was conceived during one of his mother's acts of prostitution for drugs. Eric had lived with his mother and grandmother all of his life. His grandmother gained legal guardianship of him when he was four years old because of his mother's chronic intravenous drug use.

Chief Complaint

Eric lost his mother after she fought a long battle with HIV/AIDS infection. The death of Eric's mother was unexpected because she had made a positive turn in her health during the summer with new medication and was believed to have several more years to live. However, three weeks before the beginning of the new school year, she suddenly passed away due to AIDS-related complications.

History of Chief Complaint

Eric was referred for school-based counseling because he was considered to be at risk for having academic difficulties during the school year due to his mother's death. Eric and his grandmother did receive some home-based grief counseling for several weeks following the death of his mother.

When I first met Eric's grandmother, she presented herself as a well-dressed, pleasant, and charming woman. She was primarily concerned about her grandson's well-being and his ability to perform academically given the recent loss of his mother. She reported that he had been very quiet, missed his mother, and oftentimes spent most of the day in his bedroom sleeping or staring out of the window. She reported that the grief counseling that they had done together had been helpful, but she was concerned about Eric's relationship with her since he tended to be very quiet while at home. I agreed to see Eric primarily to help him develop coping skills to successfully finish the school year and also to help improve the communication between him and his grandmother.

During the first six months following the death of his mother, he and his grandmother visited her grave site once a month to pray and put flowers on her tombstone. The grandmother said that the visits were very therapeutic for both of them and Eric agreed. He reported that he wanted to go to the graveyard more often but that he and his grandmother agreed to go once a month.

Eric was a good student and considered to be well behaved by his teachers. He was happy to have a counselor to speak with at school. During our first meeting, he asked if we would be able to play games together. This was a positive diagnostic sign because it indicated that Eric was still interested in games and hobbies. For the next few weeks, Eric and I met once a week on Tuesday mornings at his middle school. The return to school seemed to improve his mood as he enjoyed socializing with his classmates.

Hobbies

Eric informed me that he enjoyed reading race car magazines, watching television, and listening to music. He primarily watched MTV and BET music videos when he watched television. He couldn't identify a specific artist that he enjoyed watching or listening to, but he was able to identify hip-hop as his favorite type of music. He reported that he would look at car magazines during library time, but he had never bought any car magazines or had any bought for him. During our first three meetings, while playing UNO card games, Eric and I talked about his hobbies and how he was doing in class. He was very easy to speak with when the topic concerned rap music or music videos.

Course of Treatment

During our fourth meeting together, I suggested that instead of playing with cards that Eric and I do some writing together. I asked him if he had ever written a rap to his grandmother to let her know how much he loved her. He said no, so I suggested that we give it a try. He was open to the idea. I gave him the paper and we both began writing. I was surprised to see that after five minutes he had written the following:

Nana oh Nana I love you so
I hope that you know I love you so
I know that it's hard to see what you see,
it's nice to see that you read with me,
Nana,
I love you

After he read the latter rap, I applauded him and gave him a lot of positive reinforcement. I suggested that we type his rap on my computer and print it out so that he could present it to his grandmother as a surprise. He was very excited about this idea. We printed his rap out and he presented it to his grandmother that evening. She was very happy to receive the rap from her grandson. She called me the following morning to thank me for providing Eric with the guidance and counseling to write and present such a beautiful rap to her.

The following week Eric and I discussed his grandmother's reaction to his presentation. He was very happy to see how much joy his grandmother received after he presented the rap to her. He asked if we could do another rap to give her another surprise. I said of course and gave him a piece of paper and pencil. He wrote the following rap:

The sun shines every day
Warm like an apple pie
No matter how much I get sad or
No matter how much I cry
You will always be my sunshine

When the sun shines it's sometimes hot
That I am the special person you brought up
I love you with all my heart and soul
I'll love you from the North to the South Pole
Love you grandson.

As we did the preceding week, we wrote the rap on my computer and printed it for Eric to present to his grandmother that evening. His grandmother was once again touched and called to thank me the following morning. I encouraged her to use these presentations to have discussions with her grandson that she was concerned were not happening after the loss of her daughter and his mother. She said that the two had begun to talk and laugh together as a result of the raps he had presented to her. The use of writing rap helped Eric find a form of expression that was not present before he began writing to his grandmother. Furthermore, his expression to his grandmother helped her to begin feeling better following the death of her daughter, which ultimately improved Eric and his grandmother's relationship.

The following week I asked Eric if he would like to write a rap to his mother and give it to her during his next visit to her grave. He thought it was a good idea and wanted to make sure that we would be able to print the rap out. He also wanted to frame the rap and keep a copy in his bedroom. He wrote the following rap to his deceased mother:

> *This goes out to my mother*
> *Who bought my shoes that made me look gige*
> *I could never thank no one but her*
> *She was there when I was in trouble at school*
> *When I was suspended from school. . . .*
> *I got in trouble but mom was not that mad.*
> *She kept it real,*
> *Mom said stay out of trouble*
> *That's the only way to keep it real.*

I gave him positive reinforcement for the rap and we typed it and printed it for him to take home. He later reported that he was able to frame the rap and hang it in his bedroom. Furthermore, he and his grandmother took the rap to the graveyard during their next visit and he read it to his mother at her burial site. He found the experience to be very therapeutic. Likewise, his grandmother found the experience to be very inspiring. She began writing her own poetry as a coping strategy for dealing with the loss of her daughter.

23. The Case of Behavior Management

Jeremy was a thirteen-year-old boy at the time of our first meeting. His mother, who was concerned about his difficulty in managing his behavior in school and at home, brought Jeremy to my office. Furthermore, his mother was particularly interested in having Jeremy see an African American psychologist because she was in part concerned about the limited number of African American male role models in her son's life. Jeremy is biracial; his mother is African American and his father is Irish American. He had one older sister who he was very close to. The family lived in an exclusive suburb in New England. Likewise, Jeremy was enrolled in a public school that was within walking distance to his home.

Chief Complaint

My first meeting was with both Jeremy and his mother. He presented himself as a nice well-mannered boy who was energetic, inquisitive, insightful, and talkative. His mother reported that she was concerned about his ongoing difficulties in managing his behavior in school and at home.

History of Chief Complaint

At the time, a psychiatrist had been treating him with Ritalin for a diagnosis of attention deficit/hyperactivity disorder (ADHD). His mother reported he had been taking medication for two years. They noticed some beneficial effects of the medication on his behavior, but he continued to have difficulties with impulse control. The psychiatrist suggested that psychotherapy might be a helpful complement to the medication. Jeremy did not like taking the medication but thought that it was somewhat helpful.

With respect to his mother's concern about his racial identity development, she reported that she wanted to make sure that he was comfortable and secure in both his African American and Irish background. Although both parents made conscious and concerted efforts to expose their children to a variety of diverse cultural and social activities, she remained concerned about the limited number of African American male role models in his life, given that she did not have any brothers and that his school did not have any African American male teachers. Furthermore, he did not have any African American male friends because there were none in his class at school and very few close to his age living in his neighborhood. The mother's concern about his racial identity can best be described as precautionary and sensitive to the racial realities of the neighborhood in which they lived. However, Jeremy did not appear to have any major confusion or difficulties with racial issues.

Hobbies

During our first one-on-one meeting together, I assessed Jeremy's hobbies and interests. He enjoyed listened to rap music, surfing the Internet, playing video games, and playing sports such as football, basketball, and soccer. He reported that his favorite rap artists were those who combined rap with rock music, such as Limp Bizkit, Cypress Hill, and Public Enemy. We discussed these interests in detail and visited many of his favorite groups' Web pages, given his interest in surfing the Web.

Course of Treatment

Going on the Internet to check out the Web sites of his favorite groups was a great way to build a relationship with Jeremy because we incorporated several of his interests into the assessment process. Furthermore, it provided me with a great deal of insight into his interests and the veracity of these reported interests, and allowed our relationship to begin from an area of familiarity and strength, as opposed to the deficits in his behavior management abilities that precipitated his visit.

I was also able to assess if these interests held his attention for a while or if he jumped from Web site to Web site due to his limited attention span given his ADHD diagnosis. It was interesting to find out that his interest in these rap groups held his attention as we visited their Web pages. Furthermore, he was very adept at searching for information on the Internet.

With respect to his racial identity, his interest in rap groups that integrated rap and rock music was seen as an indication of a healthy racial identity development. His interest in rap and rock and diverse rap groups could be seen as his integration of the diversity within himself and his family. Furthermore, given his mother's concern about the limited number of African American males in his life, he did not appear to have any difficulties in forming a relationship with me. At the conclusion of our clinical session, I requested that Jeremy bring a copy of his favorite CD to our next session so that we could listen to it together. He agreed and we set up an appointment for the following week.

The following week he arrived with his favorite Cypress Hill and Wyclef Jean CDs. We listened to "We Live This Sh*t" and "Rap Superstar" by Cypress Hill and "Diallo" by Wyclef Jean together. He discussed why he liked these songs. It was interesting to learn that he liked the Cypress Hill songs simply for the music and the Wyclef Jean song for the content of the lyrics. We further discussed the content of the lyrics of the Wyclef Jean song, which is about the Amadu Diallo case (a case in which several white New York City police officers killed Diallo, an unarmed African student and vendor, with over forty gunshots. The killing was reportedly unprovoked and received national attention). He discussed how the Diallo case was so tragic and how he and his mother had spoken extensively about the racial discrimination of the case. Once again, he did not appear to have any difficulties or deficits in his racial identity development.

After speaking about the rap songs, he discussed how he had gotten in trouble at the school earlier that week for getting into a food fight in the cafeteria with some of his friends. We discussed strategies for managing his behavior better and how to think about the consequences of his behavior before acting. I asked him to think about this until our next meeting. Furthermore, I asked him if he thought he could write a rap about ways to manage his behavior better. He said he would give it some thought and if he could he would bring it in with him to our next meeting the following week.

The following week Jeremy arrived at my office with his mother slightly earlier than their scheduled time. His mother reported it was because he was rushing her to get to the appointment on time and that he had been speaking about how he enjoyed therapy for the entire week. He reported that he was not able to write a rap about how he could manage his behavior better. However, he did write a short narrative of some things he could do that he thought would improve his behavior management abilities. Furthermore, he reported that by thinking about the rap assignment he had not gotten into any trouble in school that week, which was the first time he had not gotten into some type of trouble for his behavior in the past five weeks.

In the narrative that he wrote, he focused on the strategies he could use to prevent him from being so impulsive. He thought it would be helpful to think about the consequences of his behavior before acting out and to avoid doing everything that his friends did while in school. He realized that oftentimes he was provoked into doing something inappropriate by another student and how he would get in trouble but the student who provoked him would not because the teacher did not see the other student's behavior. We discussed how the latter was related to basketball or football players retaliating on another player for doing something illegal during a game and how the referee oftentimes only witnesses the reaction not the initial action. After discussing the content of his narrative, I reinforced what he wrote and told him how insightful he was to come up with such good ideas. He was encouraged by the positive reinforcement. I suggested that since he was unable to write a rap during the previous week that he could try to write a rap about ways to manage his behavior while we were sitting together. He gave it a shot and after several minutes of encouragement and reinforcement he wrote the following rap:

> *Yo, to be cool count to three*
> *If you don't the outcome is worse than getting stung by a bee*
> *Don't you see*
> *To be cool you should always count to three*

What's wrong with thee
You're not listening to me
All my info is right
It might just be the tool
To keep you cool, and not in a fight.

After he read the later rap, we discussed the content and some of the factors that made him think about the value of counting to three before acting out. He reported that his mother had constantly encouraged him to count to three before acting out in school. He said his mother's comments had always gone "in one ear and out the other" until he really thought about the significance of her suggestions while writing his rap. The rap served as a catalyst for him to gain further insight into a helpful suggestion that his mother had been offering for several years. He was unable to hear or incorporate his mother's suggestions into his behavior until he listened to it through the lens of rap or writing a rap. Writing the rap about managing his behavior allowed him to put his mother's suggestion into his own words and developmental and cultural framework: rap music. I reinforced this realization and encouraged him to share it with his mother. The following week he was unable to visit my office because he had a soccer game. However, I encouraged his mother to visit so that we could discuss our progress and how she might use some of the strategies I was incorporating into our work.

The following week Jeremy's mother met with me to discuss how she could use his interest in rap music and other hobbies to reinforce his ongoing development of skills needed to manage his behavior and impulses better. We discussed his internalization of many of the messages she had been communicating to him as seen through his writings and how she could continue to reinforce this progress and contribute to further growth and development through using similar means. She began to realize that her son might not speak directly to her about some of these issues but how she could begin to understand some of the metaphors he would use to convey to her that he understood what she was trying to teach him.

I gave her some information on how his interest in sports and physical activities could be further used as an outlet for managing some of his excess energy that he appeared to be having a difficult time managing. She reported that she had modified his diet by decreasing the amount of refined sugars in his diet, feeding him only lean meats, increasing the amount of vegetables he ate, and using fruits as the primary snack food in the house for the entire family.

We also discussed how she and her husband were doing a better job with his healthy racial identity development than she thought was the case. We discussed how his racial identity development could be observed through indirect means such as the diversity in his favorite rap artists and his appreciation of lyrics in rap music that spoke to civil rights and discrimination. At the conclusion of our meeting, his mother said she would attempt to have him write another rap about other strategies that might be helpful in managing his behavior. We set up an appointment for the following week and she agreed that she would remind her son to bring in his new rap.

The following week Jeremy was unable to attend his scheduled appointment because his parents were having transportation problems due to a snowstorm. However, he and I spoke briefly on the phone and he reported that he continued to manage his impulsive behavior without incident. He reported that he had written three other raps about different ways to manage his behavior and how to handle different hypothetical situations that his mother proposed. He shared the raps with me and I reinforced his work, insight, and improvement. We made an appointment for the following week.

The following week he arrived on time and reported that he had continued to maintain the benefits of his newfound and self-imposed control over his impulsive behavior and other inappropriate behaviors influenced by his peers at school and at home. When asked why he thought he had made such a significant change in his behavior and was able to maintain the change for four weeks, he said that the constant focus on thinking about different behavior management strategies was helpful. He was also quite impressed by his ability to develop many of these coping strategies himself through his writing exercises. He also said that he began to realize that some of his friends were best to associate with after school as opposed to during school hours.

After several weeks of discussion and writing about the behaviors of his friends and his interactions with them, he began to understand that he was modeling the wrong behaviors. He was modeling their behavior of bothering other students, but unlike his friends he would always get in trouble when he tried to bother other students. He finally realized that he should have been modeling the behaviors they used to avoid getting in trouble as opposed to the behaviors that were getting him in trouble. We discussed this realization at length and he was happy that he had figured out how to use these same friends as role models for staying out of trouble.

Jeremy never brought in the other raps he wrote at home with his mother because of one reason or another. However, I continued to reinforce the skills he had developed from the exercise. After twelve weeks of treatment, Jeremy transitioned out of treatment with a newfound control over his impulsive behavior both at school and at home. He developed a greater sense of self-efficacy through his own involvement in the treatment process.

Postscript

Jeremy finished the school year without any significant behavior problems. During the final marking period of the semester, he missed the honor roll because of one C. His mother reported a significant decrease in the number of phone calls from the school complaining of his behavior. He went through the summer without any significant behavior problems at home or with his summer sports teams.

His mother reported that she was happy that she had learned how to change her view about her son listening to rap music. Although she still disapproved of him listening to certain songs that had antisocial content, she was happy that she had become more tolerant of her son's interests and had learned how to use rap music constructively to improve her communication with him.

Several factors contributed to Jeremy's improved behavior management. His use of rap music in a constructive way to begin thinking about his behavior and develop his own coping strategies, along with his mother's active involvement, his medication, and his change in diet, all appeared to work together synergistically to create a positive long-term change.

CONCLUSION

THE HIP-HOP culture and rap music have become part of mainstream America. Aspects of the hip-hop culture are presented in a variety of formats millions of times each day. Everyday life ranging from radio, television, the Internet, graffiti images, clothing, concerts, and social interactions are influenced by the culture of hip-hop. Adolescents and young adults are particularly interested in and influenced by the world of hip-hop. The culture of hip-hop can have both positive and negative influences on the lives of its fans.

Rap therapy utilizes young people's fascination with rap music to promote positive change in their lives by attempting to make antisocial thoughts and behaviors a bit more prosocial. Furthermore, rap therapy attempts to promote increased insight into the consequences of innocently accepting negative subliminal messages conveyed by the culture of hip-hop without an internal critique of the implications of accepting those messages.

Rap therapy allows clinicians, teachers, parents, and youth workers another medium through which to improve communication with young people. Once a clinician, teacher, parent, or youth worker has established a good working relationship with an individual through the use of rap therapy, he or she can begin to educate, promote greater cognitive insight, and contribute to behavioral change for the individual.

Rap music is very heterogeneous in its content. It ranges from the negativity of antisocial, sexist, racist, and misogynistic messages, to prosocial, uplifting, self-empowering, and spiritual messages. With this in mind, a child who comes into treatment and begins this type of therapy may begin by writing raps that are antisocial. However, the therapist, parent, or teacher must have a certain level of comfort with this antisocial content in order to effectively restructure the rap interest of the person with which he or she is working. By broadening the person's interest in rap music to include an appreciation of rap that is not exclusively antisocial but also includes prosocial and positive messages, one is able to utilize the person's own interests and role models to help facilitate constructive change and greater insight into his or her challenges. Once the person you are working with begins to have a greater appreciation of positive rap music, he or she can be challenged to write his or her own positive raps that focus on the issues he or she is attempting to overcome which begins the internalization process of incorporating these new cognitions into his or her behavior.

There is also great variability from song to song on a given rap artist's CD. Due to this variability, one who uses rap therapy must do his or her homework and find the positive lyrics (in a CD that the client likes) that may be hidden by the negative lyrics. A good example of a popular rap artist whose lyrics span the gamut of content from antisocial gangsta rap to prosocial rap about self-love, family, community, and self-determination is the late Tupac Shakur. Tupac's songs such as "Dear Mama," "Unconditional Love," and "Keep Your Head Up" specifically speak to listeners about the value of mother-child relationships and the importance of

African American men valuing the relationships with both their mothers in particular and women in general. If a person you are working with is a fan of the antisocial messages of Tupac, your work with him or her may begin by discussing why he or she likes these particular songs. Given this person's appreciation for Tupac, you will eventually be able to inquire about his or her thoughts of Tupac's songs that are a bit more positive. Through this discussion, the goal is to help the person begin to have a greater appreciation for the positive aspects of Tupac's music and to generalize this appreciation of positive rap music with other artists. Once the person begins to develop an appreciation for Tupac's and other rappers' positive messages, it is easy to help him or her internalize these messages and begin to change his or her behaviors.

The heterogeneity found in different rap artists' recordings can be utilized in a therapeutic way just as the specific content of a particular rap can be utilized. The diversity found in the lyrics of an artist's song speaks to the multiple identities and interests found in humanity. Furthermore, it can be utilized to help clients integrate the duality of their experiences and begin to promote an understanding of the complexity and multidimensionality of their existence in a puzzling and confusing world.

This has been utilized to help many urban youth restructure their perceptions of education and the value of school. In discussions with many urban youth, I have been challenged by their apathy toward investing in their education. Oftentimes, the clients argue from the perspective that education is worthless or inconsistent with their ideas of being street smart, hip, cool, or "chillen." However, after challenging this concept with prosocial lyrics by artists who oftentimes have antisocial lyrics, it is possible to restructure their cognitions in a way that is not possible with the lyrics of rappers who are known to rap about prosocial concepts exclusively. Thus, in many ways gangsta rap artists may have more credibility for challenging and reconstructing many urban youth's ideas.

Once young people begin to have a positive change in their thoughts and behaviors, it is important for them to maintain this positive change. This is usually done through positive reinforcement and acknowledgment of their positive change. Rap therapy has been shown to promote positive behavioral and cognitive change as is seen through the case studies presented in this book. Ultimately, rap therapy attempts to give those influenced by the culture of hip-hop more insight and different strategies to improve the quality of their lives.

Appendix A

Examples of Prosocial Rap Songs That Can Be Utilized as Educational Resources with Urban Youth

Artist	Song Title	CD	Date	Discussion Theme
LL Cool J	Big Mama	10	2002	Appreciation for grandmothers
LL Cool J	Luv You Better	10	2002	Relationships
Tupac	Dear Mama	2 Pac Greatest Hits	1998	Family relations
Tupac	Brenda Got a Baby	2 Pac Greatest Hits	1998	Infanticide
Tupac	Keep Your Head Up	2 Pac Greatest Hits	1998	Respect for women
Tupac	Unconditional Love	2 Pac Greatest Hits	1998	Family relations
Tupac	Life Goes On	2 Pac Greatest Hits	1998	Grief and loss
Tupac	Changes	2 Pac Greatest Hits	1998	Change management in the inner city
Dead Prez	Be Healthy	Let's Get Free	2000	Diet
Dead Prez	Discipline	Let's Get Free	2000	Discipline
Dead Prez	Happiness	Let's Get Free	2000	Appreciation of life
Dead Prez	Wolve's Intro	Let's Get Free	2000	Suicide through substance abuse

Artist	Song Title	CD	Date	Discussion Theme
Salt 'N' Pepa	Expression	*Black Magic*	1990	Assertiveness
Salt 'N' Pepa	Let's Talk about Sex	*Black Magic*	1990	Safe sex
Salt 'N' Pepa	I've Got AIDS	*Very Necessary*	1993	Safe sex
Boggie Down Productions	Stop the Violence	*Live Hardcore Worldwide*	1991	Violence prevention
KRS-1	False Pride	*The Sneak Attack*	2001	Humility
The Roots	Silent Treatment	*Do You Want More*	1994	Interpersonal relationships
The Roots	Sacrafice	*Phrenology*	2002	Work ethic
Digable Planets	La Femme Fetal	*Reachin*	1993	Pro-choice
Grand Puba	Proper Education	*Reel to Reel*	1992	Institutional racism
Brand Nubian	Slow Down	*One for All*	1990	Prostitution and substance abuse
Brand Nubian	Concerto in X Minor	*One for All*	1990	Institutional racism
Queen Latifah	U.N.I.T.Y.	*Black Reign*	1993	Male-Female relations
A Tribe Called Quest	The Remedy	*Get on the Bus*	1996	Personal responsibility
Outkast	Toilet Tisha	*Stankonia*	2000	Infanticide
Guru	Sights in the City	*Jazzmatazz*	1993	Navigating the city
Mos Def	Water	*Black on Both Sides*	1999	Politics
Mos Def	Mr. Nigga	*Black on Both Sides*	1999	Politics

Artist	Song Title	CD	Date	Discussion Theme
Common	Retrospect for Life	*One Day It'll All Make Sense*	1997	Responsibility of giving birth and having a child
Common	G.O.D. (Gaining One's Definition)	*One Day It'll All Make Sense*	1997	Value of spirituality
Common	Pop's Rap Part 2/Fatherhood	*One Day It'll All Make Sense*	1997	Fatherhood and parenting
Common	Come Close	*Electric Circus*	2002	Relationships
Common	Heaven Somewhere	*Electric Circus*	2002	Consequences
Talib Kweli and Hitek	Memories Live	*Reflection Eternal*	2000	Reflection and visualization of goals
Talib Kweli and Hitek	For Women	*Reflection Eternal*	2000	Issues confronted by women
Wyclef Jean	Diallo	*Ecleftic*	2000	Racial profiling
Wyclef Jean	War No More	*Masquerade*	2002	Peace without war
Wyclef Jean	Daddy	*Masquerade*	2002	Loss of father
Wyclef Jean	Knocking on Heaven's Door	*Masquerade*	2002	Loss
Wyclef Jean	Message to the Streets	*Masquerade*	2002	Children, gangs, and drugs
Sugar Hill Gang	White Lines	*Rapper's Delight*	1983	Problems of cocaine addiction
India Arie	Video	*Acoustic Soul*	2001	Self-love

Artist	Song Title	CD	Date	Discussion Theme
India Arie	Strength, Courage, and Wisdom	Acoustic Soul	2001	Maintaining inner strength and faith
India Arie	Nature	Acoustic Soul	2001	Beauty of nature
India Arie	I See God in You	Acoustic Soul	2001	Spirituality/beauty in everyone
India Arie	Beautiful	Acoustic Soul	2001	Visualization (imagery)
India Arie	Talk to Her	Voyage to India	2002	Respect for women
India Arie	Gratitude	Voyage to India	2002	Gratitude
Erykah Badu	Drama	Baduizm	1997	Use of spirituality to cope with daily stress
Erykah Badu	Tyrone	Live	1997	Female-male relations
Ja Rule	Pain Is Love [skit]	Pain Is Love	2001	Grieving
DMX	Shorty Was Da Bomb	The Great Depression	2001	Safe sex
DMX	Sometimes	The Great Depression	2001	Reflection, insight, and dichotomy
DMX	I Miss You	The Great Depression	2001	Loss, grief, memories, and journaling
DMX	The Prayer IV	The Great Depression	2001	Prayer and repentance

Artist	Song Title	CD	Date	Discussion Theme
DMX	A Minute for Your Son	*The Great Depression*	2001	Prayer, appreciation, and recognition of benefits
Cornel West	Stolen King	*Sketches of My Culture*	2001	Hope and resilience despite racism
Cornel West	Elevate Your View	*Sketches of My Culture*	2001	Black self-respect
Cornel West	N-Word	*Sketches of My Culture*	2001	Self (racial) deprivation
Ashanti	Foolish	*Ashanti*	2002	Codependence
Ashanti	Fright [over skit]	*Ashanti*	2002	Independence (ending un-healthy relationships)
Ashanti	Unfoolish	*Ashanti*	2002	Independence (ending un-healthy relationships)
Ashanti	Dreams	*Ashanti*	2002	Dreams of aspiration
Ashanti	Thank You	*Ashanti*	2002	Giving thanks
Puff Daddy with Faith Evans	I'll Be Missing You	*I'll Be Missing You*	1997	Grief
Mary J. Blige	Be Happy	*My Life*	1994	Happiness
Mary J. Blige	All That I Can Say	*Mary*	1999	Joy of love
Mary J. Blige	Your Child	*Mary*	1999	Consequence of infidelity

Artist	Song Title	CD	Date	Discussion Theme
TLC	Unpretty	*Fanmail*	1999	Self-love
Nas	I Can	*God's Son*	2002	Accomplishment
Black Eyed Peas	On My Own	*Bridging the Gap*	2000	Independence
Black Eyed Peas	Where Is the Love	*Elephunk*	2003	Unity
Black Eyed Peas	Karma	*Behind the Front*	1998	Karma

Appendix B

Online Resources On Rap Music and Hip-Hop

THE FOLLOWING is a list of a few online resources that may be helpful in identifying which songs many youth are currently listening to:

www.billboard.com	Lists the best selling rap CDs and singles. It has a category for "hot rap tracks."
www.towermusic.com	Lists the best selling rap CDs and allows you to listen to a sample of many of the songs.
www.launch.yahoo.com	Lists the most popular songs.
www.msn.com	Lists the most popular music under the music chart link.
www.bn.com	Lists the best-selling rap CDs.
www.vibe.com	Web site for *Vibe* magazine.
www.thesourceregistration.com	Web site for *The Source* magazine.
www.xxlmag.com	Web site for *XXL* magazine.
www.hip-hop.com	Features information on hip-hop.
www.hiphopsite.com	Web site featuring information on rap music and hip-hop.
www.sohh.com	An all-purpose hip-hop Web site.
www.bet.com	Web site on black entertainment.

Appendix C

Sample Curriculum of a Rap Therapy for Anger Management Group

Week 1   Introduction and overview. Pretreatment assessment of anger. What is anger? Causes of anger? Anger in the media. Anger in rap music—Tupac, "Hit 'Em Up." Snoop Doggy Dogg video clip.
Influence of anger in Rap Music on society.
Handout #1, "Some Factors That Might Contribute to Anger" (see appendix F).

Week 2   Feedback on Handout #1.
Handout #2, "Functional Analysis of Anger" (see appendix G).
Genres of rap. Heterogeneity within an artist—Tupac, "Keep Your Head Up." Politics and influence of angry rap music—Ice T, "Cop Killer."

Week 3   Feedback on Handout #2.
Handout #3, "The Relationship between Anger and Health" (see appendix H)
Video series: *From Gangsta Rap to Humanitarian Rap*, the story of Dr. Dre.
Homework: Write a rap on managing anger and rage.

Week 4   Group review of homework with feedback from psychologist and other participants.
Handout #4, "Anger Management Suggestions" (see appendix I)
Video series: *The Humanitarian and Rap* Wyclef Jean.

Homework: Write a rap on managing anger and rage, part 2.

Video About Wyclef Jean.

Week 5   Review last weeks handout on "Anger Management Suggestions"

Group review of homework with feedback from psychologist and other participants.

Handout #5, "Review Steps for Letting Go of Anger"

Feedback on functional analysis.

Music series: "Stop the Violence" by KRS-1.

Homework: Write a rap on managing behavior and anger in the community.

Week 6   Group review of homework with feedback from psychologist and other participants.

Handout #6, "Relaxation Strategies" (see appendix J)

Music series: "Be Healthy" and "Happiness" by Dead Prez.

Homework: Write a rap on anger management.

Week 7   Group review of homework with feedback from psychologist and other participants.

Feedback on functional analysis.

Music and video series: Kirk Franklin, rap and spirituality; "G.O.D. (Gaining One's Definition)" by Common.

View final scene of *Belly.*

Homework: Write a rap on anger management through spirituality.

Week 8   Group review of homework with feedback from psychologist and other participants.

Feedback on functional analysis.

Anger management through humility and personal responsibility.

Music series: "The Remedy" by A Tribe Called Quest; "False Pride" by KRS-1.

Homework: Write a rap on anger management through self-determination or humility.

Week 9   Group review of homework with feedback from psychologist and other participants.

Identifying support in family and community for managing anger.

Relapse prevention.

Dance to manage anger video series: *Rhyme and Reason*.

Homework: Write a rap on supports for managing anger and behavior.

Week 10   Group review of homework with feedback from psychologist and other participants.

Relapse prevention.

Homework: Write a rap on skills learned over the past eleven weeks.

Week 11   Certificate of completion of eleven-week anger management program.

Evaluation of program and final assessment.

Appendix D

Sample Curriculum of a Rap Therapy Empowerment Group for Women

Week 1   What does it mean to be an "empowered woman"?
         What images, media, and music challenge the image of
           an empowered woman?
         Pre-empowerment assessment

Week 2   How is empowerment influenced by how you feel
           about your appearance?
         Listen to "Video" by India Arie. Discuss the message of
           the song.
         Homework: Write a rap on self-love of appearance.

Week 3   Review homework assignment.
         What is self-esteem? How do you strengthen your self-
           esteem?
         Listen to "Respect" by Salt 'N' Pepa. Discuss the mes-
           sage of the song.
         Homework: Write a rap on self-esteem.

Week 4   Review homework assignment.
         Self-esteem, part 2. What images or lyrics challenge
           your self-esteem?
         How is esteem influenced by what others think?
         Listen to "Keep Your Head Up" by Tupac Shakur.
           Discuss the message of the song.
         Homework: Write a rap on self-esteem, part 2.

Week 5   Review homework assignment.
         How is empowerment influenced by intimacy and
           trust?

What factors make intimacy and trust difficult?

Listen to "Strength, Courage, and Wisdom" by India Arie. Discuss the meaning of the song.

Homework: Write a rap on intimacy and trust.

Week 6   Review homework assignment.

How does sexuality influence empowerment?

How do sexualized images in the media and music challenge empowerment? Do women collude with these messages?

Homework: "Continue to think about today's discussion and be prepared to further discuss next week."

Week 7   Continue discussion on sexuality, thoughts from last week.

How do sex and empowerment relate. Why is safe sex important?

Listen to "Let's Talk about Sex" by Salt 'N' Pepa

Homework: Write a rap on empowerment and safe sex.

Week 8   Review homework assignment.

Empowerment with female-male relationships.

Listen to "U.N.I.T.Y." by Queen Latifah.

Homework: Write a rap on empowerment and relationships.

Week 9   Review homework assignment.

Empowerment and work.

Discuss issues related to empowerment through work.

Week 10   Final group.

Postempowerment assessment.

Final thoughts.

Appendix E

Sample Curriculum of an Adolescent Boys Psychoeducational Group

THIS WILL be a psychoeducational group. The purpose of the group is to review and teach adolescent boys about a variety of topics they have reported would help them transition into late adolescence and early adulthood. The group will utilize rap music as a medium of communication and teaching to help the participants internalize the relevance of each of the weekly topics. The group will run for eight weeks.

Week 1   Introduction and overview. Assessment of rap music's influence on the lives of the participants.

Week 2   Taking responsibility.
          Listen to and share thoughts on "The Remedy" by A Tribe Called Quest.
          Homework: Write a rap on how you take responsibility for your life.

Week 3   Review assignment from last week.
          Managing peer pressure.
          Listen to and share thoughts on "Discipline" by Dead Prez.
          Homework: Write a rap on how you manage peer pressure.

Week 4   Review assignment from last week.
          Avoiding drugs.
          Listen to and share thoughts on "Wolve's Intro" by Dead Prez.

> Homework: Write a rap on how you avoid drugs in the community.

Week 5 Review assignment from last week.
Respect for women.
Listen to and share thoughts on "Keep your Head Up" by Tupac Shakur.
Listen to and share thoughts on "U.N.I.T.Y." by Queen Latifah.
Homework: Write a rap on respect for women.

Week 6 Review assignment from last week.
Relationships and sex.
Listen to and share thoughts on "Let's Talk about Sex" by Salt 'N' Pepa
Listen to and share thoughts on "Shorty Was Da Bomb" by DMX.
Homework: Write a rap on the importance of safe sex.

Week 7 Review assignment from last week.
Racial profiling.
Listen to and share thoughts on "Diallo" by Wyclef Jean.
Homework: Write a rap on how you plan to manage racial profiling.

Week 8 Review assignment from last week.
Maintaining a healthy diet.
Listen to and share thoughts on "Diet" by Dead Prez.
Homework: Write a rap on how you plan to maintain a healthy diet.

Week 9 Review assignment from last week.
Final thoughts on the group.
Certificate of completion.

Appendix F

Some Factors That Might Contribute to Anger

MANY DIFFERENT factors or stressors can lead to feelings of anger. Some of the following stressors may contribute to feelings of anger. Review the following list and identify any of these factors that make you angry. At the end of the list, please list the factors that make you angry. It is important to identify which factors make you angry, since everyone experiences anger for different reasons.

Frustration
Unemployment
Poverty
Feelings of limited control
Loud noises
Traffic congestion
Stressful situations
Resentment
Fear
Difficulty sleeping

List the factors that make you angry to gain a better understanding of your own personal triggers:

_____

_____

_____

_____

_____

_____

Appendix G

Functional Analysis of Anger

Date	Antecedents	Behavior	Maintaining Variables (Secondary Gains)	Consequences	Alternative Strategy

Appendix H

The Relationship Between Anger and Health

Uncontrolled anger is positively correlated with many health problems. Some health issues that can be exacerbated by anger include:

Headaches
Increase in blood pressure
Insomnia
Increased risk of substance use
Muscle tension
Heart attacks

Please list any health issues that affect you as a result of your anger:

_____   _____

_____   _____

_____   _____

_____   _____

Appendix I

Anger Management Suggestions

Several factors can help you manage anger effectively. Points to keep in mind as you attempt to manage your anger include:

- Develop insight into the factors that make you angry.
- Learn how your body responds as you are getting angry. Does your jaw tighten up? Does your heart start to race? Do you clench your fists? By learning how your body responds to feelings of anger, you can gain further insight into the onset of angry emotions and respond appropriately before your anger takes control of you.
- Develop alternative strategies for managing anger that are productive and do not exacerbate your anger. They might include:

  Exercise
  Deep breathing
  Visualization
  Meditation
  Writing about your feelings
  Speaking with an understanding friend
  Humor

- Learn how to become assertive. Many people get angry because they do things they do not want to do. Since they continually do things that are against their will, they progressively become more and more frustrated, which can eventually lead to to an explosion of anger. It is better to be assertive and decline to do some of the things you don't want to do.
- Try not to take things personally.

These are just a few strategies that may be helpful in your pursuit to regain control over your anger.

Appendix J

Relaxation Strategies

There are several strategies you can use to help you relax when you feel angry emotions coming on. Some strategies that may be helpful include:

Meditation
Deep breathing
Visualization
Muscle relaxation

Think of which one works best for you.

Index